ULTIMATE SUCCESS

Connecting with Your Multidimensional Self and Your Longing for Happiness

ULTIMATE SUCCESS

7 Secrets to Spiritually-Based Leadership

Anneli Driessen Ph.D, CMS, MCC
CEO Coach

National Library of Canada Cataloguing in Publication Data

Driessen, Anneli, 1950-
Ultimate success! : seven secrets of spiritually-based leadership : connecting with your multidimensional self and your longing for happiness

Includes bibliographical references and index.
ISBN 0-9689843-0-4

COVER DESIGN: Jim Bisakowski, Desktop Publishing Ltd.
TYPESETTING: Jean Robinson
PRINTED IN CANADA BY FRIESENS

PUBLISHED BY
Anneli Driessen
1516 Louise Place
Victoria, BC, Canada V8P 2T9
Tel. 250-472-0909
Fax 250-721-4296
anneli@annelicoach.com
http://www.annelicoach.com

ENDORSEMENTS

"This is a book that has something for everyone. Anneli's ideas have application whether you are a CEO or a stay-at-home mom."

Joan Johnston,
Vice President, Johnston & Culberson, Inc.
Seattle, WA, USA

"... I believe that you were directed to send the book to me not because you needed my feedback, but because I needed to read it. You can't begin to imagine the world of good it did for me... "

Flavio Veiga,
President and CEO, Circulo Dos Professionals De Vendas
Curitiba, Brazil

"Everyone talks about "thinking outside the box," but few actually do. This is one of the few books I have read recently that challenged me and expanded my vision of what is possible.

As a psychologist, it concerns me that so many of the writers of popular business books seem to have little background or understanding of human psychology. Anneli Driessen, herself a psychologist, brings much wisdom and insight to discussions of important interpersonal issues in business.

If you are ready to have your mind stretched and your vision of the World expanded, I highly recommend ***Ultimate Success!*** *Even if you do not agree with all of her concepts and views, I am still certain you will gain much value from this unique book on leadership."*

Donald Moine, Ph.D. Business and Sales Psychologist, Author 'Unlimited Selling Power,' Palos Verdes, CA, USA

"This book speaks powerfully and passionately to leaders as well as Coaches. Leaders will receive insight about themselves and guidance for incorporating spirituality into their lives and their work. Coaches will receive insight about leaders and how to become more powerful and effective Coaches, from the inside out."

Fran Fisher, MCC
President and CEO, Academy for Coach Training
Bellevue, WA, USA

"Rarely do you find a discussion of the role of Spirit in our personal and professional lives that is grounded in realistic, concrete and easy to understand language. In this book, Anneli Driessen uses her personal life experience and her extensive work as a Coach for CEOs as a foundation to achieve clarity. She aids the reader by highlighting the key points at the end of each chapter."

Rey A. Carr, Ph.D.
President and CEO, Peer Resources
Victoria, BC, Canada

"Anneli Driessen is a listener, a seeker, a Soul intent on sharing her beliefs in the hope of helping others who struggle with the big questions of life. This book is a gift to others who are searching."

Price Pritchett, Ph.D.
Chairman and CEO, Pritchett, LLC
Plano, TX, USA

"Anneli Driessen opens her readers to a sense of beauty and truth; a sense of helping the morally good in people by appealing to the choices that life offers, while aspiring to eternal happiness through an inquiry toward the existence of God.

Doctor Driessen's capability is to help individuals have a clear conviction that they are born with purpose. She invites us to commit ourselves in our professions, our leadership roles and interpersonal relationships to make an authentic effort to protect our World."

Alfredo Castillo Ramírez
President and CEO, JAK & MEX Consultoria
Lima, Peru

"Anneli has much life experience and shares her viewpoint in a very stimulating and thought provoking manner. This book sets a very positive tone for business and leadership practices."

Jock Mc Keen MD and Bennet Wong MD,
Partners of PD Seminars
Gabriola Island, BC, Canada

"This book is highly stimulating, informative and innovative. It widens the horizons and will help all those in search for a new orientation to find their ways and to master their future."

Professor Dr. Phil. Dr. Theol. Peter Antes
President of the International Association for the History of Religions
University of Hannover, Hannover, Germany

"This book is excellent. It will nourish your mind and nurture your Soul. It's loaded with useful knowledge and substantial wisdom for anyone who wants to grow personally and professionally."

Nido R. Qubein
Chairman, Great Harvest Bread Company
Founder, National Speakers Association Foundation
High Point, NC, USA

"With pin-point accuracy, you identify the "prime mover" of the leadership thought and action process. Humans are, first and foremost, spiritual beings. While "wired for sound" from the God-world, many of us have our receiver turned off. The flow of creative ideas, ultimate meaning, joy and fulfillment in life is short-circuited by our ignorance about things spiritual.

You help to flip the switch back on!"

Joseph Ellis
President and CEO, The Ellis Group
Redmond, WA, USA

"In my work as an Executive Speech Coach, I find my clients are seeking more understanding of themselves and how they can lead their companies in uncertain times. I will definitely recommend Dr. Driessen's thoughtful book. Many of the questions today's leaders are struggling with can be answered."

Patricia Fripp, CSP, CPAE
Author 'Get What You Want,' Executive Speech Coach
San Francisco, CA, USA

ENDORSEMENTS

"Dr. Driessen has engagingly and skillfully put forth the notion a successful CEO can and must eventually enjoy a marriage between practical business skills with creative intuition and a spiritual awakening... Only then, can we awaken to our multi-dimensional nature and move into our highest octave of consciousness."

Lee Pulos, Ph.D., ABPP
Board Certified Diplomate in Clinical Psychology
Vancouver, BC, Canada

"This book will give you the confidence to walk your talk, to understand how to be on the ladder of success and find that your ladder is actually leaning against the right building when you get to the top. True fulfillment comes from a rich inner life that is centered on spirituality.

This book will give you tools, ideas and reasons how and why an integrated spiritual life helps everyone in the new wave of doing business."

Ilona Selke
Author 'Journey to the Center of Creation,' Researcher
Pahoa, HI, USA

"Anneli expanded my corporate vision to a panoramic view by carefully and thoughtfully leading me through a process of self discovery that allowed me to easily see business solutions that had formerly lurked behind brick walls."

Raymond C. Horton, LLC
President & CEO, Horton Financial Services
Shreveport, LA, USA

"Many executives and other individuals will benefit from your book. The human race has advanced substantially during these last 1000 years; however, spirituality still remains in the dark ages.

I congratulate you in your pursuit of the truth and universal well-being. Good luck in your commitment to touch people who are willing to reach a higher level of consciousness and purpose."

Jeffrey Abrahams,
Partner, TASA do Brasil — Consultants in Executive Search
Sao Paulo, Brazil

"I know I seek guidance from forces I don't understand, sometimes, many times within the same day. This is a business book that puts the entire package together and I highly recommend it."

Susan DiFlorio
GM, Focal Communication Corp. of Washington
Seattle, WA, USA

"The underlying message of this book is a wise, helpful one: through attention to our spiritual side, we will be more fully evolved human beings — beings that can serve our communities and planet Earth as well as joyful and fulfilled individuals.

Dr. Driessen's many examples and references to philosophers, psychologists, scientists and even Spirit Guides provide lots of food for thought and further explorations."

Leslie Campbell
President, Campbell Communications Inc.
Founder, *Focus on Women* magazine
Victoria, BC, Canada

*"**Ultimate Success** provides light on the values that have long resided in the shadows of my thoughts. A thought-provoking message from one who understands... Anneli Driessen."*

Herb Knoll
Corporate Executive, Author/Columnist
Longwood, FL, USA

*"Dr. Driessen's **Ultimate Success – 7 Secrets to Spiritually-based Leadership** reveals the impact that "being true to ourselves" has on life and on people. Dr. Driessen shares with us the value of understanding and living our core purpose."*

Kirby Fox
CEO and Founder, Excell Executive Leadership Exchange
Portland, OR, USA

*"Dr. Anneli Driessen's analysis of current business activities and the need for spirituality and integrity is indeed timely. Dr. Driessen's book **Ultimate Success — 7 Secrets to Spiritually-based Leadership** addresses and explains spiritual management and life success in a way that leads each reader to an enriched life.*

This book has made a positive difference in my business practices and in my personal life."

James L. Watson
Senior Vice President, National American Insurance Company
Austin, TX, USA

To all the people in the World who are committed to a life of purpose, service and integrity.

Prejudices, preconceived opinions and beliefs always stand in the way of true wisdom. Conceited opinions are always suicidal in their influences. They bar the door to the entrance of truth.

Ralph Waldo Trine, *In Tune With The Infinite,*
first published in 1899

ACKNOWLEDGMENT

It is without exaggeration that I acknowledge the hundreds of very special people who greatly contributed to my personal and professional development. Since listing every one by name would fill over ten pages and since each one of you knows who you are, from my heart to yours, please accept my gratitude for your loving support.

Thank you my closest friends, **Liz James, Lorna Holmes, Ruth Mohacsi, Manuela Matthias, Gloria Lintermans, Annette Wall** and my first dance teacher, **Marga Benner-Roye.** I have felt your love and care more than from anyone else in my life. I want to specially thank **Gerri Knilans** for her excellent editing assistance.

In addition, the following people have played a vital role in my personal and professional development. They taught me about values and helped me in their own unique way to successfully take my next step in life: **Prof. Dr. Eugene Eunesko, Rudolf Zierholz, Prof. Dr. Peter Antes, Dr. Bill Downe, Dr. Reeta Sanatani, Louise Hay, Drs. Jock McKeen** and **Bennet Wong, Judy** and **Randy Revell, Dr. Lee Pulos, Lisbeth Marcher** and **Jack Chriswell, CSE,** perhaps one of the most humble, competent and loving leaders in the World.

Thank you, **Dad.** You moved on to God in 1976. I feel the deepest gratitude for the gifts you bestowed on me. You modeled commitment, perseverance, beauty, good will, humor and excellence for me. You always believed in me.

Thank you my dearest friend, **Roy Chitwood, CSP, CSE,** for your support, guidance and mentoring during many of my adult years. I know I am not easy at times, particularly when you refer to me as a "pain in the brain." I know you genuinely love me.

Anneli Driessen
Summer 2002

Table of Contents

INTRODUCTION

This book is my loving invitation to successfully fulfill your human experience, gain inner peace and find your way back to God. For me, this means to experience full participation, integrity, respect, joy, belonging, beauty, inspiration and zest as well as abundant love and faith in all areas and in every moment of life.

My goal in writing *ULTIMATE SUCCESS!* is to create a short, condensed summary of the many lessons I have learned from working with successful business people — leaders in the private sector as well as in government and other large organizations — and to provide an autobiographical perspective about my quest for life's purpose. The information and insights shared in this book come from my personal learning experiences and from my work as a clinical therapist and CEO Coach.

In today's World, which has been plagued by crime and corruption and with the unprecedented terrorist destruction of the World Trade Centers in New York on September 11th and the war that is affecting the entire globe, we are more than ever confronted with fundamental choices about our purpose and personal conduct. The reality is that harmony begins from within. There is a core learning process we all share as human beings, and that is to connect with ourselves and to stay on our path. The key issues in this process are faith, the right action and an exploration of self. This means first recognizing who we "really" are, what our unique purpose is and then proceeding with great courage and integrity.

The degree of comfort or acceptance, however, of that spiritual journey is very different for each of us. Some people resist this journey for their entire lives, seeking only material goods, status and fame. These people are spiritually narrow-minded and say, "What you see is what you get!" or "When you are gone, you're gone, and that is the end of that."

Thankfully, most people are intuitively aware that there is something else. Even if they are struggling, they are on a spiritual path. I've learned that often times what we commonly call depression is really the inner struggle of the Soul. There is a solution to this struggle. It is to embrace the knowledge culled from a worldwide spiritual awakening.

This book is going to best serve those of you who fundamentally agree that there is one God or Creator, regardless of your religion or belief system. To get real value, you will need to be open to the fact that life goes on after our physical death. And perhaps most importantly, you need to have an inherent belief that you are on this Earth to learn and return to God. If you are open to these concepts, you will get significant value from reading this book. If this does not resonate with you, I invite you to continue reading anyway and to make room in your mind for new and different perspectives.

I will also address subjects of spiritual crisis, God, Life in the Universe, Spirit and extraterrestrial existence. While these may be foreign subjects to you, I know of their existence and feel confident that, should you choose to continue reading, you will gain new knowledge.

No matter what your life experience has been so far or what your karmic destination is this time around, you must be committed to doing the best that you can. This begins with a leap of faith. How do you do this? By making a DECISION to have faith! It is that simple. There is no magic or trick involved.

ULTIMATE SUCCESS! is a roadmap to finding peace of mind and a sense of serenity, to healing your soul issues and living without fear... to being so convinced of the "rightness" of who you are and of your connection to this Universe that you just know that everything is as it should be, even when life circumstances seem otherwise. *ULTIMATE SUCCESS!* is also being spiritually connected to our earthly planet, which is your crucial contribution to World Peace. Only through our inner journey can we wholeheartedly commit to healthy relationships, truly ethical business practices and the protection of our environment.

The knowledge I share with you in this book comes not only from what I have learned personally but also from my personal spirit guide. This phase of my spiritual journey began in 1994. I responded to a newspaper article, which led me to read two books: *From The Beyond (Volumes One and Two),* written by the American medium, Eva Hermann and published in German, my native language. Having studied Gustav Jung, Sigmund Freud, Aldous Huxley, Teilhard de Chardin and Thomas Mann, I knew there was no way that this woman with only a basic high school education could have used their terminology, language and conceptual knowledge firsthand. I was profoundly affected by the depth of the information she provided.

In her books, both spiritually transmitted to Ms. Hermann, these former scientists and philosophers corrected and added to their theories from their perspective from the Beyond. For example, in one passage the Spirit entity of the former scientist Aldous Huxley emerged. Once world-renowned for his research on LSD, he shared his deepest regrets for having misled people with his findings because of his own need for fame and recognition. Teresa von Avila, Hildegard von Bingen and Winston Churchill also wrote through Eva Hermann. I was so deeply touched and excited by her work that I searched for over a year to find her books in English so that I could share this information with my closest friends. In the end, however, I was unsuccessful.

Then, in early 1995, I came across an ad in the German publication, *Esotera. (Esotera* is probably the largest esoteric publication in Germany and has been in existence for at least 30 years.) A "spiritual study group" was looking for new members. The ad read, "Only positive thinking and sincere seekers (not fanatics) need apply. A quality (writing) medium transmitting correct information from the Beyond will be available." The ad also mentioned that this study group was not linked to any religion, sect or other spiritual organization.

At that time I had already studied para-psychological phenomena for many years because of my genuine interest in finding insights into the secrets of the Universe. Noticing this innocuous ad was interesting in itself because I usually didn't pay any attention to the advertising section of this publication. Now that I have a greater understanding of how our Spirit Guides and other invisible helpers influence us at all times, I know that I had been "directed" to find it.

The ad referenced Eva Hermann, along with three other authors: Nowotny, Kardec and Greber. I didn't have much access to German literature from my hometown in Victoria, BC, on Canada's West Coast, so I jumped at the chance to make a connection with this group. I wrote a letter to introduce myself. I explained that I lived in Canada and would not be able to join their study group; however, I asked if they would send a list of recommended reading materials. After hearing nothing for two months, I finally received a letter. It was from an elderly gentleman by the name of Mr. Alfred Lamy.

He wrote a very formal, yet very sweet letter giving me the name of my Spirit Guide. Mr. Lamy talked about faith and about me. It was such a loving and caring letter from a stranger that I started to cry. I was stunned. I intuitively knew that he was genuine. No telephone number was included with the letter, but I finally found a listing in the telephone directory. I called him, and we have stayed in touch ever since.

Shortly thereafter I received a notice from Alaska Airlines that I had to use up my frequent flyer miles or I would lose them. I thought to myself, "Nothing happens haphazardly, but who in the world would want to fly to Germany in the middle of a cold, wet November?" I did. When I arrived, I telephoned Mr. Lamy to suggest a meeting. He was excited, almost ecstatic, to hear that I had come to visit. I wasn't really sure what he was all about, but I was intrigued and looked forward to meeting him.

I had already rented a car for the four-hour drive, but he urged me to take the train instead. His suggestion seemed silly, but for some reason I followed his advice. I took the train, and he met me at the station. I later found out that there had been several major car accidents on the Autobahn. I would never have arrived on time if I had driven. There he stood at the train station, adorned with a bow tie and an armful of yellow roses. It was obvious that he was a gentleman. He had a little yellow car that looked like it was almost ready to fall apart. At that point, I was curious and honestly just a little amused. We drove to a beautiful, isolated small restaurant where he had more fresh flowers waiting. He treated me like a queen, and I was very flattered.

With his huge, penetrating eyes, he checked me out. He wanted to learn everything about me. Having spent over forty years studying spiritual phenomenon, he was well read and very knowledgeable. He explained that he had been asked by a Spirit Entity ("Theobald") to put that ad in the *Esotera* magazine so that I would respond.

Theobald is a Spirit Guide who writes messages through his medium, Manuela. (Manuela herself does not give any personal advice. She serves strictly as a channel.) As we talked, my excitement and curiosity grew. He began to unroll cylinders of old wallpaper on which the medium Manuela had written in very large script — backwards and upside down in non-stop sentences. I had previously witnessed a wide range of mediumistic transmissions, but never before had I seen anything like this.

After dining, we were off again, this time to visit a Hungarian family-style restaurant where Manuela lived and worked as a cook. Surprisingly, I was not the least bit skeptical at that point. In fact, I found it all very interesting. I was totally open and accepting of what was happening.

Manuela was in her early forties and quite overweight. She was very kind and very, very shy. She did not look anything like what one might think a medium looks like (whatever that is).

Prior to my departure from Canada, Mr. Lamy asked me to prepare a list of written questions about my life issues to which I sought answers. He advised me to take the time to think about these carefully and develop my questions in a precise and clear manner. I came prepared with close to 50 questions, some of which included, "What is the purpose of my life? Why am I here? Why am I visiting you? What is going on in my personal relationships? What should I do in my business and with my health?" "Where is my (deceased) father now?"

Theobald, through his medium Manuela, answered all of my questions accurately and specifically. The script was now as small as normal handwriting. I was fascinated by the speed with which Manuela wrote the answers from right to left and upside down on the back of scrap paper. Theobald "wrote" in non-stop sentences, with all the words running into one another. After each answer, Manuela paused and read it out loud. I was so intensely focused that I could actually feel my heart beating rapidly. I knew in the depths of my heart that everything "he" told me was right. I believed, I was being exposed to the most comprehensive, most loving source of information possible. My doubts would come later.

It wasn't until I was on my way home to Canada that I started to think, "Anneli, you're crazy — traveling all that way to Germany looking for answers to some of the most important universal questions from people who, in the traditional sense, were fairly uneducated." Even using my frequent flyer mileages, the trip was expensive, so future trips would be out of the question. In addition, there were plenty of mediums in Canada. And what kind of a Spirit was Theobald anyway? Maybe the Theobald phenomenon and the experience were all a fake. Maybe he was just an earthbound Spirit who wanted to make himself important. My doubts grew, one on top of another, and for the next six months, I questioned everything.

After I returned to Victoria, Manuela bought a fax machine, and that's when everything began to change. My questions and Manuela/Theobald's answers flowed between our two machines — questions and answers about the Spirit World, Angels, about the different levels of Angels, what this work is all about, and more. I was still not convinced totally, but I could not, would not, stop the flow of information. I was consumed by this communication. It felt like I had been given the KEY to secret knowledge.

Determined to make up my mind about the sincerity and quality of this information, I decided to return to Germany and live with Manuela's family for nearly one month. Even with doubts and extreme caution, I intuitively knew that this trip would impact my future in a significant way. I was determined that, by the time my visit was over, I would know 100 percent whether I was committed to further involvement or not.

Living with the family, I worked right alongside Manuela and her family in the restaurant. I delivered food at night to their customers and helped clean the restaurant in the morning. I was the driver when we bought groceries, and I even shoveled dog poop from their balcony. I loved it! I watched, listened and learned as the townspeople, and sometimes others, who came from different parts of Germany, consulted with Theobald through Manuela — all looking for answers to their problems. I continued to ask my own questions very carefully because I did not want to offend Manuela. I couldn't help but think: if this spiritual work was so utterly important, why had Theobald chosen this little town and Manuela, a woman with such a simple, yet hard life? After carefully formulating my questions, I was told that I *would understand later, when I had matured more spiritually, and that the spiritual journey is about effort. If it were easy, God could just give us the correct lotto numbers, for example, and we would have two thousand believers in a week.* ***Proof would come after faith, not before.***

I returned to Canada firmly entrenched in the knowledge there is a God, there are uncountable and unimaginable life forms throughout the Universe, and there are past lives. I ached for more answers, thinking, THERE IS SO MUCH TO KNOW! It was humbling, frustrating, even disheartening for me to realize that there is so much more we will never know because of our primitive, limited human brains.

My knowledge and understanding are not ideas I want or need to defend. However, if one accepts the basic fact there is a God, this book could be a useful tool for those who want to find their way back to God. God exists.

You will find the most value in this book when you are emotionally, spiritually and intellectually open to the ever-expanding knowledge available, when you recognize the existence of your spiritual Source and Creator, God, and are committed to *positive* and *good* as ever-increasing forces of true happiness and success.

How do I know? Consider this sampling of Theobald's messages about God taken from hundreds of pages of transmitted information:

1. *God is the Creator of the Universe, of all Life and all visible and invisible matter. He is eternal, non-material, unchanging, unique, almighty and the sovereign of good and justice. He is Truth, Light and Love.*
2. *Man is incapable of comprehending and defining God.*
3. *The earthly Life and Death of Man will remain a secret, which will not be revealed to him until after his transition to the Beyond.*
4. *God loves every human equally.*
5. *Man is one of God's many uncountable creations.*
6. *All creations are a part of God.*
7. *God gives life and determines the transition and continuation of each Soul/Spirit entity.*
8. *Man differs from animal through his consciousness, his free will, his immortal, incarnated Spirit and his individuality.*

9. *The development and evolution of spiritual consciousness is never ending. It continues after the Spirit is one again with God.*
10. *The purpose of life is to school the Soul/Spirit for the return to God.*
11. *God teaches the Law of Karma, or cause and effect. It is multidimensional.*
12. *God created the Laws of Nature.*
13. *God's Laws are eternal.*
14. ***Man has freedom of action. He alone decides his future. God gave him this ability and opportunity so that he can determine the exact direction of his life and not feel victimized when things don't go well. God gave the gift of full accountability.***

After completion of this book I wrote to Theobald and asked for his feedback. In summarizing his message to you, the reader, he wrote: *"After reading this book you will understand more what it really means to have and live by FAITH. You will understand the true magic that comes from understanding "flow" as a process of the circular nature of energy that occurs conscious or unconsciously. You will know that the secret to your success requires you to let go of the negative and then allowing the positive energy to flow back to you, just like a boomerang.*

The deepening knowledge and understanding about this phenomenon is the KEY to your personal destiny."

Remember the purpose of this book is not to convince you. Its purpose is to help you to develop courage, to receive validation, to be truly successful and to make your life a bit easier. I am not an

Evangelist, Preacher or New Age Guru. I am a Coach.

Before reading ahead, please take time to review the Glossary. By doing so, it will help you gain an understanding of many of the important terms and people that have played such an important role in my, and hopefully your, *ULTIMATE SUCCESS*.

Glossary of Definitions and Concepts

My unusual, privileged, personal and professional exposure to individuals and organizations in the public and private sector and the Spirit World has allowed me to gain unique insight and perspective on life, which I am sharing here as a friend and Coach. In order to make it easier for the reader to assimilate and understand the perspective from which I write, I am placing the Glossary at the front of the book rather than at the end as traditionally done.

The impact on my life of my special contact with the Spirit World has been profound. With this context I will blend references from the Spirit World and age-old wisdom with modern knowledge and invite the reader to recognize the connection to universal principles.

Universal Laws

As humans, we can only speculate on how the Universe originated. There is agreement, however, that there is order in the Universe. "Order" is defined in Webster's New World Dictionary as "conformity to law," and "orderly" is defined as "well managed."

Recognized for their multidimensionality and connection, the following are some of most commonly known Universal or Cosmic Laws:

- *The Law of "As Above, So Below"*

  Macrocosm and microcosm are governed by the same organizing principles. Everything within us reflects with the Universe. Inner and outer, above and below, converge within the individual. The center of the Universe is within you and is everywhere.

- *The Law of Correspondence*

  Everything is interdependent and yet participates in the integrity of the whole while recognizing the interrelationship between organisms and their environment.

- *The Law of Karma*

  "What goes around comes around." The Sanskrit (ancient language of India) word for action is Karma. This Law refers to action and the effects of action, cause and effect, which bring about cosmic justice. It is multidimensional and non-linear.

- *The Law of Mentalism*

  "All is mind." This law describes the creative force of thought, from which all things — events and words — first take seed. Thought is the underlying, causative principle and resource from which we create reality.

- *The Law of Polarity*

  This is the law of the dualistic nature of things — the principle of opposites. It supports simultaneously the existence of positive and negative, hot and cold, black and white and masculine and feminine. Each element has two poles, which is sometimes perceived as an apparent paradox.

- *The Law of Rhythm*

  Rhythm is the measure of motion that occurs between

the two poles established by the Law of Polarity. The Universe, and everything in it, is rhythmic. Life itself is a rhythmic process, full of time sequences, repetition and recurrent cycles. Rhythm is organized vibration.

- *The Law of Spirals*

  Spirals are symbols of eternity, a spherical vortex or funnel with their centers perpetually alternating. While Cosmic Laws govern all manifestations, they appear to move within spiral patterns of time or other types of intervals. These occur in harmonically repeating cycles of creation and destruction as well as expansion and contraction.

- *The Law of Vibration*

  Nothing rests. The Universe and everything that exists are in constant motion.

VIBRATION

Vibration is the very fast interchange between energy and matter, which creates movement. Every entity has its own, unique vibration.

Vibration also goes far beyond our visible physical body. We are hybrids of species, made of both matter and spirit. We are multi-dimensional, and we usually do not have much, if any, memory of our many parts while in our current human existence.

The concept of the Soul is a little bit different. It is physical and of matter like our visible body, but much less condensed. After our transition to the Spirit World, some of the more sensitive humans can still see these Soul bodies at times on lower levels.

The vibrations in our Soul bodies change, just as they change in our physical bodies. For our physical bodies, this change is particularly obvious as we age. But there is an aspect of the Self, the Spirit, which is non-physical and is a part of our original source, God. It was always there and will continue to exist into eternity.

The Phenomenon of Mediums and Spirits

Even though known, recognized and documented worldwide for thousands of years, the phenomenon of Mediums and Spirits is still a mystery and is highly controversial for most people. A Medium is an individual who "channels" one or several Spirit entities. A good Medium typically doesn't give personal advice and is usually a very humble person — certainly not someone who is accumulating material wealth as a result of his or her gift. A quality Medium intuitively knows who needs help but may not be able to pay and offers his or her gift anyway.

It is important to learn how to distinguish between both quality Mediums and quality Spirit entities, since there are sometimes gifted Mediums channeling negative or non-quality Spirits without knowing it. In addition there are also those Spirits who are not particularly advanced or knowledgeable. They tend to give people just the information they want to hear such as when an individual will meet the man of her dreams, find a job, etc. or they communicate repeatedly the same ongoing series of messages about love, beauty and peace without any useful content or help for humans. Therefore, it is wise to discern the information transmitted and to understand that this common kind of communication is relatively meaningless in one's spiritual evolution and higher spiritual development.

Most important, quality Mediums or Spirit entities will never disclose information about anything that interferes with one's Karma, learning process or personal decision making. Nor will they communicate when someone will die.

Example: "Theobald"

"Theobald" is the name of a Spirit entity that writes messages from the Beyond through his medium, Manuela. Theobald is an "Information Spirit," a channel into the Spirit World. Not unlike a telephone line, "he" transmits messages to us from the Beyond through Manuela. He has permission and the ability to retrieve all of his information from a source, which he refers to as "The Multidimensional Brain."

His purpose is to give information to those people who search for truth, direction and assistance. Theobald makes it very clear he is *not* a fortuneteller and that his contributions are *not* meant to serve sensationalism, exploitation or any other needs of superficial Spirit entertainment.

To date he has transmitted many messages to us from the "Multidimensional Brain" relating to issues and secrets about our existence on this planet and in the Universe. This material has been documented and recorded for over 15 years. Students who have compared it with many other spiritually transmitted messages from the Beyond have concluded that the quality, consistency and simplicity of this material by far surpasses that of any previously recorded documentation.

Example: Manuela

Manuela is a woman in her forties who lives with her family near Munich, Germany. She has had the ability to deal with the Spirit World since early childhood. Manuela does not counsel people or give any personal advice; she serves strictly as a channel. Since 1986, she has been "Theobald`s" exclusive Medium only.

As a child, Manuela was unaware that no one else saw what she saw. She grew up alone, without siblings. She was a quiet child because she learned that when she talked about what she saw, people thought she was crazy.

Manuela was also quiet in school, but not because she didn't understand things. She knew all the answers but wouldn't speak out. Actually, Manuela was bored, so she doodled and daydreamed while talking and playing in her head with her Spirit friends. Outside of the school grounds, she met many of them at the garbage dump, where they often asked her to find books and to look for specific things. Her parents would find her digging around in the dump and punish their "weird" child. Yet to her, Spirits were quite normal.

Manuela also wrote not knowing at the time that it

was the Spirits writing. Her parents gave her old receipt books. She wrote on the backs of pages, although she couldn't read what she wrote because she was too young at the time. Today she wishes she still had those earlier writings, but unfortunately, her parents threw out everything years ago.

She was always searching. Years later, as an adult, Manuela became involved in a research program and once again began to write, but this time in a research setting. During these years, while he was still alive, Theobald was part of the research team. Several different Spirits wrote through her as well. After Theobald`s death, she began working exclusively for Theobald. Then she began to doubt what she was doing and stopped writing. She thought, "Maybe I am making it up. Maybe it's only coming from my subconscious."

Manuela didn't "write," i.e., *channel,* again for a year and a half, until one of her former clients came to her, begging her to channel once again. When she did, she wrote backwards and upside down for the first time. She has since learned that her hand was guided to do this for her own protection.

At the beginning, Manuela had many premonitions about individual and global events. Realizing she couldn't do anything about it, she just allowed herself be aware of this information and let it go. She never passes along this knowledge because she knows that everything that happens is supposed to occur without her interference.

Manuela is a most remarkable woman. Although shy, her willingness to give of herself, at times, to exhaustion is amazing. Like other good mediums, she cannot ask for herself, so it is up to us to look after her.

The Konzern

The Konzern consists of groups of people dedicated to intellectual and spiritual development throughout the World. They voluntarily come together to fulfill a common goal. Theobald chose the word "Konzern" because the magnitude of this work on the economic and political environment could be compared with the multi-international companies in our World. The term "Konzern" is simply a working term and could be replaced by "Multidimensional Community" or another similar term.

The purpose of these non-denominational and non-political groups is to support, educate and facilitate the personal advancement of all individuals who are sincerely seeking knowledge, inner contentment and meaning. They most often gather in so-called round-table discussion groups called "Tabula Spiritualis" throughout the World addressing a wide variety of topics as they relate to us as spiritual beings.

The Konzern is not a religion or sect. It is about education, teaching and self-study. People are encouraged to be open-minded and to trust their own judgment and intuition in formulating their ideas. The initiative for this communication came from the Beyond in order to provide information about the Universe. It was not sought after by the Medium or anybody else.

According to Theobald, *"The highest goal of the*

Konzern is to save those Souls who, unfortunately, have gone astray from God during the past millions of years and are now on their own. These are Souls who denied the existence of God or who simply refused to deal with His existence. The Konzern's aim is to fill the Universe with human Souls who are pure — to have a Universe ruled by peace and harmony, love and intelligence. It is to ensure that Satan, with his unrecognized, enormous power, will no longer have a chance to gain control."

PART I
THE SUCCESSFUL CEO

Chapter 1
SPIRITUALITY IN BUSINESS

> *The place of spirituality, or religion, in the workplace has always been a sticky, often taboo, subject. It's a personal issue, and most business leaders are content to leave the idea of God in the company parking lot. They can pick Him (or Her) up again on the way home. There are signs, however, that spirituality — which usually conveys a broader meaning than religion — is taking on more meaning and importance in executive suites. At the least, it's being talked about more....*
>
> Jim Braham, "The Spiritual Side,"
> *Industry Week,* February 1999

It is not news that the highest spiritual values and principles guide long-term success in today's business environment. What does not work long-term is to be one person at work and another person away from the office. What value is there to only want and live for material goods, financial power and beating the competition at all costs?

India's spiritual leader, Sathya Sai Baba, says that fundamental human values, concern for well being, responsibility, love, truth and inner peace, provide the foundation for every major spiritual tradition. The following fundamental human values also directly support established business values:

- Concern for well-being fosters great service, trust and quality.
- Truthfulness fosters honest relationships, collaboration and courage.
- Equanimity fosters creativity and wise decisions.

Spirituality-based principles are old and yet today are a growing trend in both the private and public sector. Sai Baba says, “It is the vision of service and a servant leader that can touch us deeply and draw us away from self-serving agendas.” Typically, a major self-serving agenda of a dysfunctional business is greed. The major self-serving agenda of a dysfunctional public sector organization is power. Both are fundamental distortions. Leadership as a calling involves a noble motivation and a powerful vision. Therefore, effective leaders strive to integrate personal and spiritual values into the workplace. They work to stimulate quantum leaps in creativity, process improvement, customer service and other business values.

Consider the example of Jack Kahl’s, CEO of Manco, Inc., based in Avon, Ohio, a developer and distributor of Duck-brand tapes. While his leadership style is based more on inspirational deeds and sayings from business and sports, he acknowledges that spirituality plays the primary role in his life. “All things in business are based on trust, and your relationship with God is all about surrendering to somebody greater than yourself. Surrender your will to God," says Kahl. "Live within His house, and you'll have a good life. More important, you'll have a better life after this one."

God-consciousness is not necessarily dependent on your religious framework. Five years ago Krishan Kalra was, by his own admission, one of Silicon Valley's "cutthroat CEOs," interested primarily in amassing great wealth. While the founder and CEO of BioGenex Laboratories Inc. was prospering financially, his marriage was failing, and his children were alienated. This led Kalra to recall childhood memories from India where, even in poverty, he once had a strong connection to his Creator. He decided to take a three-month leave from work to immerse himself in the Bhagavad-Gita, one of Hinduism's major sacred scriptures.

Now Kalra's marriage and home life are healthy. His San Ramon, California, company, which develops, manufactures and markets molecular and cellular diagnostic systems used to detect cancer and other diseases, is thriving. He attributes his renewed perspective on life to reconnecting with his Hindu spiritual roots, the Bhagavad-Gita in particular.

"One major way to attain the divine is called karma yoga. This means that whatever I'm doing as a CEO, my primary objective is to do it for the divine, meaning society," Kalra explains. "As a result, my focus is first to be the best CEO, ahead of making a lot of money. Money is a by-product. As a result of this, I have no fear of failure, and I can take risks. I am much more composed, at ease and relaxed," says the 50-

something executive. Kalra sees no conflict between his spiritual and business life. In fact, he believes spirituality keeps him "grounded," returning him to "home position." Every morning when he closes his eyes, he totally disconnects from his work and says this simple prayer: "Lord, I am at your service. What is it you want me to do? Lead my way."

Jeffrey H. Coors, president and CEO of ACX Technologies, Inc. also believes in the role of spirituality in business. He says, "You can be good, righteous people in the workplace and conduct your affairs in a righteous manner without getting overly religious or threatening. But I'm very open about my faith with fellow employees. I regularly talk about the fact that we are created in God's image and that He has given us free will, but that our duty is to respect others. I encourage people to be all that God created, the best you can be. In fact, I actually think you can prosper better as a company if God is your focal point."

A de-spirited organization can *function* despite the drain of its spiritual and emotional capital. How? Unfortunately, it learns to cope by creating rigid control structures, rules and regulations that bring out the worst of human nature. According to Alberto Villoldo, Ph.D., medical anthropologist and director of the Four Winds Society, "Things appear to be running smoothly until a new challenge arises (e.g., a change in the business climate) threatens the company's success and seems insurmountable. Yet when we heed our emotional and spiritual guidance, we can change the world. We can rewrite our job description instead of changing jobs. We can discover maps that lead us to landscapes we never dreamed possible before."

A spiritual organization will nurture the Souls of the people who work for it in order to achieve *genuine* success. Further, it recognizes all the dimensions of our lives need to be included to be truly fulfilled. We must have the desire and make the effort, every day, to *really* connect with our inner Self and God in order to experience deeper meaning and greater understanding.

Key Points

- **The highest spiritual values and principles guide long-term success in today's business environment.**

- **Effective leaders strive to integrate personal and spiritual values into the workplace to stimulate quantum leaps in creativity, process improvement, customer service and other business values.**

- **A spiritual organization will nurture the souls of the people who work for it in order to achieve genuine success.**

- **Make the effort, *every day,* to really connect with your inner Self and God.**

PART I
THE SUCCESSFUL CEO

Chapter 2
THE DILEMMA OF THE CEO PERSONALITY

> *The acts of men, who have come out to serve or lead, have always been misunderstood since the beginning of the World and none can help it.*
>
> Mohandas Karamchand (Mahatma) Gandhi

In my many years of working with people, particularly with senior level executives and CEOs, I have discovered that people in key leadership positions belong to the most misunderstood professional group on this planet. I have come to *realistically* appreciate their unique situations, strengths, multiple talents and competencies, visions, perseverance and courage. I have also learned about their particular kinds of stress, pressures, frustrations, distrust (and sometimes paranoia), challenges, questions, worries and sleepless nights. I've discovered their fears, doubts, pain, fatigue, hopelessness and even depression. I know what they are talking about when they complain they've lost the "fire in their belly."

Their days are extraordinarily FULL. Not only do they need to keep up with what is going on in their own industries but they also need to be aware of global business trends and political issues. They are expected to sit on numerous advisory boards, be readily available to the media and make continually tangible contributions to their community. True privacy is rare. As Jack Welch, longtime CEO of General Electric Co., said in an interview with the New York Times, he wants to "retire and only then work 40 hours per week."

Top executives need to discern new information quickly and make decisions accordingly. Yet this is not enough. These supermen and superwomen are continually questioned and challenged by their executive boards, employees, and yes, even by their spouses, children and extended family. Their leadership is evaluated constantly — and mostly criticized.

Often called "narcissistic," they tend to isolate themselves and not readily listen to anyone. Generally, they are not easily emotionally accessible, and because they are commonly so self-absorbed, they have little desire for advice or support from any other source. CEOs tend to be emotionally distant and highly distrustful. Because of their extreme independence and self-protectiveness, it can be difficult for anyone to get close to them. Therefore, once they have become a CEO, mentoring of any kind is likely to be a particularly challenging task. A Therapist, Mentor or Coach must demonstrate an extraordinarily profound understanding and empathy for the CEO's feelings, perceptions and resistance in order to gain his or her trust. My experience has taught me that once there is a trusted bond with the Coach, CEOs are willing to share an emotional and intellectual intimacy.

Today's business leaders have a significantly higher visibility and profile than ever before. They are more often in the limelight. Many have appeared on radio and TV and have even published their own success stories.

CEOs are innovators with a tremendous drive to succeed, independent and not easily impressed by anyone or anything. They are experts in their industries but also have a more global perspective. They are the ones who generally pose the critical questions. They want to learn with a nearly insatiable hunger everything about anything that affects their company. For the most part, they want to be respected — not loved.

To paraphrase George Bernard Shaw, some people see things as they are and ask why; CEOs see things that never were and ask why not? CEOs see the big picture, but they are not analyzers who break down big questions into manageable problems; nor are they "number crunchers." They try to extrapolate in order to understand the future as they wish to create it.

Successful CEOs have vision, but vision alone is not enough. The simplest definition of a CEO or leader is someone whom other people follow. In fact, CEOs must be able to attract followers. They need to demonstrate personal magnetism and the ability to lead while generating enthusiasm.

Even when people respond positively to the typical CEO personality, there are potential dangers. Charisma is a double-edged sword. It fosters both closeness and isolation. As he or she becomes increasingly self-assured, the CEO becomes more spontaneous and feels free of constraints. Ideas flow, some good and some not so good. They may evolve to believe they are invincible. Rather than trying to persuade those who disagree with them, they feel justified in ignoring them, thereby creating further isolation.

Despite the warm feelings their charisma can evoke in others, CEOs are generally not comfortable with their own emotions. Given their difficulty with knowing or acknowledging their own feelings, they are uncomfortable with other people expressing theirs. Therefore, they tend to only pay attention to and listen to the kind of information they seek.

This is one explanation of why CEOs do not want to know what people think of them, unless not knowing is causing them a real problem. Being extraordinarily sensitive, they don't tolerate dissent very well and often do not listen when they feel threatened or attacked. As a typical CEO might bluntly put it, "I didn't get here by listening to people! If I listened to my employees' needs and demands, they would eat me alive."

CEOs are acutely sensitive and aware of whether or not people are with them wholeheartedly. They know whom they can use, and they can be brutally exploitative. This lack of empathy and their extreme need for independence make CEOs look relentless and ruthless in their pursuit of victory. There is a kind of emotional intelligence associated with empathy and genuine interest; however, CEOs often rely more on their instinct and on "street smarts" than on actual people knowledge.

In my work with CEOs, I have discovered that their most secret and deepest desire is to really understand others — their styles, motives, strengths and weaknesses. These are areas where they value guidance and direction from a competent Coach they can safely confide in and trust.

Key Points

- **People in leadership positions belong to the most misunderstood professional group on this planet.**
- **Often called "narcissistic," CEOs tend to isolate themselves and not listen to anyone.**
- **Trusting anyone is difficult for CEOs. But once trust is earned, they will engage in a close, intimate working relationship with their Coach.**
- **Despite the warm feelings their charisma can evoke in others, CEOs are typically not comfortable with their own emotions.**
- **The CEO's most secret and deepest desire is to really understand others — their styles, motives, strengths and weaknesses.**

PART I
THE SUCCESSFUL CEO

Chapter 3
The Old and New Paradigm

The words "New Millennium" have been used so much that they have almost lost their impact. Nevertheless, this book would not be complete without suggesting the following contextual shifts that impact all business strategies:

OLD/ ***Newtonian***	**NEW/** ***Quantum Physics: Einstein***
• separate departments	• whole systems
• optimize departments	• optimize the whole
• decisions top down	• decision making on all levels
• training specialty	• cross functional
• people static	• creative/moving/dynamic
• inflexible	• flexible
• bigger is better	• smaller is better
• primary purpose: profit for shareholders	• primary purpose: profit community, individual, company

New trends in schools of management, as well as the nationwide establishment of professional task forces, confirm that spiritual work practices do belong in today's corporate arena. Metaphysical and spiritual management methods have increased production, improved sales and enhanced morale and corporate success. For example, Montreal canned-food magnate J. Robert Quimet thinks he has found the way to make his employees happier and more productive. His prescription? A heavy dose of silence, humility and prayer.

In his book, *The Ethics of Excellence,* Price Pritchett, Ph.D. and Chairman/CEO of Pritchett & Associates, Inc. (a Dallas, Texas-based firm specializing in mergers and organizational change) outlines a framework for business excellence. The following paragraphs encapsulate his key messages:

"Excellence in business now calls for character... integrity... fairness... honesty... a determination to do what's right. There are high ethical standards across the board. Work gives life meaning. Purpose. It contributes to our sense of worth... our self-concept... even our mental and physical health. Work helps keep us centered (grounded), and that's so valuable during these times of chaotic change. But here's the paradox: The only way our work can carry this kind of positive, steadying influence in our day-to-day lives is for us to keep changing our approach to the job. As the world evolves, so must we. Our work will slowly destroy us if we don't update our methods and mindset."

Pritchett identifies four options for handling change: we can cope with, adept to, or exploit change or we can actually create change on purpose. People operating at the first level of change (coping) respond with a 'victim mentality.' They feel helpless and are pessimistic and dependent. Valuable energy is invested in resistance, anger, blaming or fear. These people focus on problems instead of solutions. They talk about how hard things are and the reasons why they can't make it work. Usually the mindset is to wait and hope for a so-called 'return to normal.'

People at the second level of change display more of an 'adjustment mentality,' according to Dr. Pritchett. Here there is an effort made to adapt to the new situation. Some energy is spent on accommodating the change with a 'cut your losses and go with the flow' attitude. They are less damaging to the organization; however, little personal effort is put into positively driving the change.

At the third level of change is the 'opportunity mentality.' The mindset is to exploit change. The investment is in a search for positive benefits primarily for oneself and then toward the contribution of energy and attention to the company's cause.

At the fourth level is a 'possibilities mentality.' Here people are proactive, not reactive. Rather than waiting for change to happen, they make it happen. Not content with coping, adapting to, or even exploiting change, they are creating it. At this forth level, says Pritchett: "*The company gains a competitive advantage. It's both energizing and fun to be the architect of your own future —* ***to move with initiative, imagination and a true sense of urgency with a mindset of purpose, adventure, optimism and faith.*** *At level four, you don't fight the future, you partner with the world of tomorrow and co-create change. Level four is the success zone. Migrate there, and you can meet the*

21st Century on its own terms."

This is really what the secret to business and successful living is all about. It's not just about making money. It is also about making life happen, making good things happen for other people and making sound contributions to the community, country and the World. As Roy Chitwood, former President and Chairman of Sales and Marketing Executives International said in his inauguration address: "The business of life is living, but nothing happens until somebody gives something."

Key Points

- **Metaphysical and spiritual management methods have increased production, improved sales, enhanced morale and corporate success.**
- **It's both energizing and fun to be the architect of your own future.**
- **Business and successful living are about making money, but they are also about making life happen, making good things happen for other people and making sound contributions to the community, country and the World.**

PART I
THE SUCCESSFUL CEO

Chapter 4
INTEGRATING SPIRITUALITY IN BUSINESS AND AT HOME

If I hear the word 'spirituality' one more time, I'm going to throw up... Anyway, I don't even know what 'spirituality' means.

Anonymous

Build bridges, not walls. Start in your own backyard. Your relationship with yourself begins with recognizing your strengths and weaknesses, making a commitment to ethical values, examining attitudes and building a personal definition of standards. These are vital in order to be successful in business and to make a difference to others. This means defining and redefining who we are. It is only after we grow stronger that we as individuals can reach out and give to other individuals, communities and nations.

Peter Koestenbaum, author of *The Image of Man,* is a well-known clinical philosopher. He lectures extensively on courage and greatness and why these principles are so important in business today. According to Koestenbaum, "Setting goals and defining what you want to do within a certain time is good, but sometimes it doesn't go far enough. We forget to ask the question: Why am I doing this? Is it just to put bread on the table, to achieve wealth or to become famous? Or is there some other motive, which is a driving force inside of us?"

In his teachings, he addresses issues relating to all of us such as birth, death, evil, fear, freedom and love. He believes that addressing these issues and demonstrating the courage to deal with them constructively will achieve greatness in business.

Albert Einstein, Buckminster Fuller, Fritjof Capra, Peter Russell, Gary Zukav, Joseph Campbell and many more internationally recognized scientists have dared to go a step beyond their discipline and reach for the big picture — the laws and principles that wisely underlie or govern life itself. They have become mystics, philosophers and theologians. Yet in their life's work, they have all come to the same conclusions:

1. Everything — absolutely everything — organic, or what is still commonly called inorganic matter, is made of the same *basic stuff.*
2. All planetary evolution is developing towards some overall *good* (improvement, wellness).
3. There is a supreme force, intelligence, law or God, which is *eternal.*
4. This force, intelligence, law or God is within *everything.*

This means that to serve and to help is necessary to achieve success. As we work day-by-day, even in the smallest, most invisible way, we make a difference on a much larger scale.

How do we do this? By understanding what is now happening in the universe requires a higher order of logic than the intellect can create. It requires heart. We must turn within, to the evolution of our Soul. We must first be willing to be open to new information in order to make a choice to pursue the path of the heart. To pursue this path, we must first learn to be *still,* and that requires discipline and determination. Only with this practice, in combination with all our cognitive insights and decisions about ourselves, our goals and visions, will we obtain that ever-growing sense of comprehending who we are and why we are here.

Aligning ourselves in daily life with our evolving, authentic selves will lead to a much deeper understanding of what our personal and professional wellness is all about. It takes courage and greatness to be truly successful. The word courage contains the French word *Coeur* or heart. When you come from the heart, you cannot help but experience integrity, authenticity, greatness and love. Although difficult to put into words, here is my favorite quote of true love:

Love
Is omni-inclusive,
progressively exquisite,
understanding and tender
and compassionately attuned
to other than the self.

Buckminster Fuller

What does this have to do with business? What does

it *not* have to do with business! Building bridges means recognizing yourself and others and connecting consciously from a perspective of goodwill, love and respect. From a metaphysical perspective, we need to do nothing but learn our own lessons. From a worldly place, listen, encourage, acknowledge and reinforce. This is how we build bridges in business.

Take a moment now to think about the following six important questions:

1. What is my business?
2. What is my overall reason, purpose, mission, reason for being?
3. What am I now doing for myself physically, emotionally, socially, intellectually and spiritually?
4. What am I now doing to build bridges?
5. What changes am I willing to make?
6. Of what am I proud, and for what will I acknowledge myself?

Picture a World full of people, committed to liberating themselves from anything that is not in alignment with what is most important to them. Imagine people who have the desire, determination and commitment to their own evolutionary process that will enable them to become strong individuals who make a difference! Think about those people who choose to make an important contribution to this planet.

William C. Miller, an internationally recognized speaker and expert on innovation, believes the goal of all mystical spiritual traditions is to realize our inherent

Oneness with our Creator. He says, "We are born of creation and share in its creative powers. From Oneness with God, we co-create with God in this world. Work is the opportunity to deepen and express an experience of Oneness with all beings through selfless service. While the notion of selfless service flies in the face of our normal desires and beliefs about compensation and benefits programs, it is one way to begin experiencing the true nature of God as one's own nature, purified through more and more selflessness. The intrinsic motivator, our inner nature of love, is the very nature of divinity and the very life principle behind all organisms, including organizations."

Connect *first* with yourself, and then the business will follow. Learn how to listen to your employees, to put policies in place that really service your employees, customers and other business associates. Ultimately, this is what leads to a spiritual, albeit mostly intuitive, understanding of a much bigger and worthwhile goal.

Key Points

- **Build bridges, not walls. Start in your own backyard with your relationship with yourself by recognizing your strengths and weaknesses. Make a commitment to ethical values, to examine attitudes and build a personal definition of standards.**

- **Turn within, to the evolution of your Soul. Be open to new information in order to make a choice to pursue the path of the heart. Learn to be *still.***

- **When you come from the heart, you cannot help but experience integrity, authenticity, greatness and love.**

- **From a metaphysical perspective, we need to do nothing but learn our own lessons. From a worldly place, listen, encourage, acknowledge and reinforce. This is how we build bridges in business.**

PART I
THE SUCCESSFUL CEO

Chapter 5
Good Strategies, Practices and Habits

Too many folks want the body of Schwarzenegger without getting out of bed!

Dr. Laura Slessinger

On the plus side, CEOs actively encourage their people to challenge their ideas. In his book, *The Five Temptations of a CEO: A Leadership Fable,* Executive Coach and Consultant Patrick Lencioni says, "Trust them (your employees) with your reputation and your ego. As a CEO, this is the greatest level of trust that you can give." Lencioni suggests five temptations a CEO must learn to overcome, and in return, people will respond with respect and honesty.

- Choose trust over invulnerability.
- Choose conflict over harmony.
- Choose clarity over certainty.
- Choose accountability over popularity.
- Choose results over status.

Yet CEOs who focus on results more than status, accountability more than popularity, clarity more than certainty, productive conflict more than harmony and trust more than invulnerability can still fail if they don't stay grounded and spiritually connected. Only by instilling trust and confidence, which are rooted in faith, can executives have the courage to engage in productive conflict.

It is evident that the attitude and genuine compassion demonstrated toward fellow workers, superiors and subordinates have a positive effect on personal and organizational success. Leaders are more effective when they transmit a broad, enduring and spiritual purpose. It is highly questionable that a CEO can truly serve his or her customers and employees without having a basic spiritual (although not necessarily an organized religious) connection. More and more, emerging leaders are finding the courage to bring the benefits of spirituality into the workplace. While acknowledging the need to refrain from trying to convince anyone else how to think, they still bring to the workplace the principles of spirituality whether in good times or times of crisis.

For example, one CEO of a large manufacturing company based in Atlanta, GA tells his employees that it is more important to set priorities to be a good father, husband and member of the community than to focus on work. By doing this, he creates an environment that allows everyone to exercise his or her own spiritual beliefs, whatever they may be.

Ultimately this kind of CEO is more successful because he recognizes that long-term success is based on values such as integrity, being in alignment in thought, word and deed. No one can possibly be fully successful in business without also applying these same principles at home to their relationships with their spouses, children and friends. Using different principles in different places and for different situations will eventually create discord within our bodies and minds, causing stress, anxiety and ultimately, illness.

To be fully physically, emotionally and mentally healthy, to really have a sense of inner-happiness, it is necessary to be totally authentic in every way. Doing the "right" thing (whatever that is for you) is doing what is honorable, positive and just. You will recognize your authentic Self because it will resonate well within your heart. Here are four recommendations for accomplishing this goal:

1. Find and rely upon a competent Coach as your confidant.

For example, CEOs generally speaking love their spouses. Often the marriage provides a sense of comfort, mental vacation and enjoyable companionship. Yet it is almost as if their partners are living on another planet. CEOs often withhold entire parts of themselves from their spouses. Sharing information about job related stress, such as financial pressures and high-risk situations are typically, are not possible with a spouse without causing worry or concern. It is also inappropriate for a CEO to talk with members of their board of directors or senior executives about certain issues since these people often have their own political agendas. In addition, it might be perceived as weakness if the leader suddenly were to share personal concerns with them. A top-notch, competent

Coach will serve as an ideal advisor, friend, mentor and confidant.

To have someone with whom one can feel safe to discuss hidden fears, someone who understands or at least intuitively assesses and comprehends the complexity of a CEO's work, is an enormous gift and most valuable asset. Acknowledging areas of fear and being open to finding a quality coach or mentor may not only be a wise business investment but can also be crucial in times of personal crisis. Even though we are ultimately alone with our life choices, it is unnecessary to wallow in loneliness or to struggle alone. By allowing ourselves this kind of personal support, we can enjoy even greater energy and stronger resilience.

2. Hold brief meditations daily.

There is a powerful, yet quiet spiritual retreat movement sweeping the entire Western World. People need to escape from their hectic lives and claim time for inner reflection, in solitude or in small groups of like-minded individuals. People of all denominations and other religious traditions, are rediscovering old practices largely lost in today's World. Retreats are flourishing. Despite its trendy appearance, however, the retreat as a movement has a solid core of authenticity. Those who participate take the time for spiritual or soul renewal very seriously.

Faith is important to people, even while their feelings towards organized religion may have become ambivalent. In a peaceful, quiet environment we are totally looked after and can concentrate without worrying about food, phone calls, or other outside interferences. At retreats, we don't even have to talk! Not only are successful people taking time out for personal renewal more often, but they have also learned the excellent practice of taking a period of time each day to turn inward. This does not have to be complicated nor does it require much time. Simply be mentally with your God, Spirit Guide or Guardian Angel. You don't need to be in a special place, sit in an awkward meditative position, sing a mantra or light a candle. Even though these kinds of rituals can be pleasant for you personally, God values your sincerity and honesty more.

One CEO I know has a very ill child. The first thing he does in the morning is feed his little son, which needs to be done in an unusual way because of the child's multiple disabilities. The CEO told me this is his most precious time of the day to "connect with God" and say his prayers.

Another CEO diligently completes a fast, 40-minute walk every morning. As he walks, he becomes "clear and ready" for the day. Others read spiritual scriptures and other inspirational writings, write in their personal journals or sit on their front porches with their morning coffee and quietly listen to music. Whatever helps people to connect with God is the right way.

Being quiet can be a learned ability. There are a number of good techniques available, which might make this experience a bit easier for some. This book is not about techniques. Those can be acquired through Self-Hypnosis, Transcendental Meditation, Autogenic Training, Guided Imagery and certain kinds of Yoga. Depending upon your personal preference, use what works best for you. Just remember this does not have to turn into some profound gesture or major physical exercise. Just do it first thing in the morning, and do it regularly. The key is to have quiet time on a *consistent* basis, ideally at approximately the same time daily.

If we fail to focus inward for a few moments every day because we are running late, traveling or just sleeping in, we will notice it. We quickly become more frazzled and prone to anxiety and won't be as effective or levelheaded. It is the day-to-day consistency that is important. Its value builds over time and will ensure the male and female principles within us are in balance during every kind of business activity. Masculine principles typically involve strategic planning, goal setting and execution of assignments. The female principles have to do more with creativity and intuition, which include spiritual expression, nurturing and encouragement. Both are equally necessary for the successful executive.

3. Move your body and develop a sense of humor.

The body is precious. Move it more than from your car to your office. The reality is that CEOs who take care of themselves in even the simplest ways tend to be the most productive and have a good chance for longevity. Simple walking is recognized as one of the most natural and effective forms of movement. In addition to choosing a personal confidant, practicing self-reflection and moving their bodies, successful people are also likely to be more open, likable and good-humored.

Productive people have perspective. They are able to detach themselves and laugh at their irrational needs. Although serious about achieving their goals, they are also playful. As leaders, they are aware of being performers. A sense of humor helps them to maintain enough perspective and humility to keep on learning.

4. Protect yourself from negative Spirits.

It is also important to self-protect from negative Spirits. The conviction that Spirits influence or possess people is based on the assumption that *"life continues after death."* For centuries, possession has been documented in numerous case studies and shown us that we are immortal beings. Only the physical body dies, and something else, which we call the Soul or Spirit, survives.

Earthbound Spirits are simply those who did not make the natural transition to their next higher planes of existence and may need our help to get there. Our world appears to be populated by disincarnates as well as by living human beings. Disincarnates can be denied entrance by keeping our own energy fields vibrating at a rapid frequency.

Certain gifted people, such as clairvoyants and a wide range of Mediums, are able to see Spirits, auras and other energy forms, which are invisible to us. They can "read" a person's state of health, emotions and a great deal more from the aura's shape, density and color. For example, anger sends out murky red "arrows" that penetrate another's aura and impact their well-being.

Fortunately, a lot can be done to prevent Spirits from attaching to humans. The *key* to protection from Spirit intrusion is to keep one's aura strong. Strengthen the aura by using the "White Light" technique. Ideally, use it routinely (twice a day) before getting out of bed in the morning and again before going to bed at night. The more this technique is used, the more resilience you will have, and the stronger your aura will become. This "White Light" technique takes only a few seconds to perform. It can be done anywhere and without any time-consuming preparation.

The "White Light" Technique

Using your creative imagination, imagine the crown of your head opening, allowing a bright light from above to enter and fill your entire body, all the way down to your toes. Once you are filled with this light, allow it to form a strong radiant wall of White Light that completely surrounds and protects you from any negativity or harm.

Once you learn and practice this immensely powerful technique, you will be able to use it with just a thought, and instantly you will be protected.

The vibrations of our energy fields also vary constantly. These vibrations reflect one's general state of being — one's physical, mental, emotional and spiritual state. Emotions such as anger, depression, fear and envy are all poisons that change the color of one's aura and slow it down. When confronted with any situation or person involving negativity, surround yourself with "White Light."

It is imperative to keep yourself and your environment as positive as possible. Strive to create a balance of work, play and rest, because Spirits can enter a weakened aura as easily as someone can walk through an open door. In addition, in order to protect yourself, it is a good idea to avoid recreational drugs and alcohol. Getting "stoned" or drunk even once can result in a possession that can last a lifetime!

Possessions can also occur more easily after surgery or during hospitalization. Again, use the "White Light" technique often. Use it from the time you enter the hospital, throughout your stay, immediately before anesthesia and as consciousness is regained. Stay as relaxed and positive as possible while in the hospital.

At funerals (and at all events associated with death), if viewing the body, mentally instruct the deceased to look for loved ones and to go to the Light. Tell them they are safe and loved, and that they will be fine. Send them extra light from the Beyond, as well.

Prayers are *very* helpful. They call upon powerful sources of the Highest Light Beings. Even doctors often enlist the aid of spiritual healers. The Lord's Prayer is a potent means of protection. The 23rd Psalm is also excellent for this purpose. Say both of these prayers, and you will not only raise your aura's vibrations, but also attract help. If you are a non-Christian, say any prayer or affirmation with which you feel comfortable. If you feel you are dealing with a demonic entity, then seek the help of a credentialed and competent hypnotherapist who has special skills in "Spirit Releasement Therapy."

It is also important to protect your home from negative spirits.

1. Do *not invite Spirits* in with séances, the Ouija board or automatic writing. These activities can easily create potential disasters that may outweigh any possible benefits.
2. Avoid excessive use of drugs or alcohol.
3. Surround your home *daily* with White Light. Imagine each room filled with "White Light." It takes less than a minute.
4. *Firmly* tell disturbing Spirits to leave.
5. Ask mentally for protection from Higher Light Beings such as Jesus, Spirit Guides, your Guardian Angel or God.
6. Keep your home happy and filled with love. Negative Spirits feed on the energy from negative thinking.

Having negative, earthbound or ignorant spirits in your home is *not* a catastrophe, but these entities can be irritating. Spirits are a "natural" occurrence, and *you can* deal with them *yourself.*

Key Points

- **CEOs who focus on results more than status, accountability more than popularity, clarity more than certainty, productive conflict more than harmony, and trust more than invulnerability can still fail if they don't stay grounded and spiritually connected.**

- **To be able to discuss hidden fears with someone with whom you feel safe, someone who understands or at least intuitively assesses and comprehends the complexity of a CEO's work is an enormous gift and most valuable asset.**

- **Claim time for inner reflection, in solitude or in small groups of like-minded individuals. Give yourself quiet time on a *consistent* basis, ideally at approximately the same time daily.**

- **Protect your energy fields from negative vibrations and/or Spirits with "White Light."**

Summary of 4 Key Recommendations For Good Practices and Habits:

1. *Find and rely upon a competent Coach as your confidant.*
2. *Hold brief meditations daily.*
3. *Move your body and develop a sense of humor.*
4. *Protect yourself from negative Spirits.*

PART I
THE SUCCESSFUL CEO

Chapter 6
CEO COACHING

Coaching is like having a personal trainer for your Soul

Rey A. Carr

Personal coaching, once a little known option for career and personal enhancement, is skyrocketing in popularity and acceptance, even among CEOs and other top-level executives. In an unpredictable and volatile global economy, business leaders are faced with unique challenges and tough decisions. Accordingly, the demand for credible and qualified coaching professionals will undoubtedly continue to increase.

To realize the value and potential of CEO Coaching requires a clear understanding of what it is, what it addresses, and most importantly, what it can accomplish. Fundamentally, coaching is a service that involves a special one-on-one relationship between an individual and a professional Coach. A Coach assists the client in clarifying, articulating, prioritizing and achieving personal and professional goals. It is a collaborative and innovative process.

It is important to distinguish coaching from therapy. The line between the two is often blurred as many of the necessary skills in both disciplines are shared. Unlike traditional therapy, however, coaching is more about focusing on positive results and solutions rather than dealing with crisis and issues relating to clinical pathology. Due to its positive focus, coaching helps to overcome obstacles, difficult circumstances and resistance. Coaching is NOT a quick fix, a trendy buzzword or a "flavor-of-the-month." It is a cost-effective and valuable catalyst for both personal and business transformation.

In coaching relationships, CEOs and senior executives typically address sensitive personal or personnel issues, production problems, business etiquette, implementation of change or specific challenges, for example, in sales and marketing. They also work with intra-personal issues such as burnout and loss of enthusiasm or interest, which are inappropriate to share with their peers and, sometimes, even with their spouses. A CEO's decision to work with a Coach is intimate, personal and totally confidential. It is based upon the integrity of both people involved. If the client is willing to be absolutely open, honest and to offer complete disclosure, the results can be staggering.

The International Coach Federation (ICF) reports that in 1999 the number of Coaches jumped from 5,000 to close to 20,000. This is both good and bad. Today, an executive has many Coaches from which to choose, but their qualifications and credibility vary significantly.

If looking for a Coach, what steps can you take to

ensure the best possible selection? The most important steps are to review a Coach's credentials, life and work experience and skills. Anyone can call himself or herself a "Coach," and there is an increasing number of "wannabes," "flakes" and false-prophets trying to cash-in on the recent growth of this new profession. To avoid making a poor choice, it is important to check references. In addition, trust your intuition. The whole basis for the coaching relationship is one of trust. Most Coaches offer complimentary engagement conversations. During this time, you have the opportunity to build rapport and make your decision.

Many executives choose to work with a Master Certified Coach (MCC) who is certified by the International Coach Federation (ICF). The ICF certifies Coaches who meet or exceed clearly defined standards and competencies. A Master Certified Coach (MCC), for example, must abide by a strict Code of Ethics and Standards of Conduct, be able to document at least 200 hours of coaching-specific training, 20 hours of individual mentoring and supply at least 10 client references. In addition, he or she must document at least 2,500 coaching client hours and must have passed a written and oral exam. A certified Coach, however, is still not a guarantee for quality and competency.

On its web site, *www.coachfederation.org,* the ICF provides a list of Coaches along with their specialties. Accessing this list allows an individual to make a preliminary selection and send out a request for a proposal. Fees will vary widely depending on the terms of engagement, experience, credentials, references and frequency of coaching sessions. The average contract runs six months and may subsequently turn into an ongoing retainer relationship.

Almost all coaching is done through a combination of phone calls, e-mails, video and Internet conferencing. Modern technology dramatically increases the odds of finding the right Coach, since the selection is not limited to one's immediate geographical area. In fact, in many cases, Coaches may not even meet their clients in person. Despite the lack of face-to-face contact, coaching clients who work remotely often report the ability to generate more intimacy and do more than (they would) if coaching sessions were conducted in person. Why? The level of focus, energy and effort are at a peak. A lot can be accomplished in 30 minutes. Coaching by phone is very efficient. The small talk and lingering conversation often present during person-to-person meetings is eliminated.

Given the uniqueness of the CEOs personality profile, it may be difficult to find a suitable match. CEOs typically work with consultants on special areas of expertise, but not with Coaches. In my experience, personal recommendations through a highly regarded business associate, for example another CEO, seem to be most successful. The following scenario reconstructs a conversation that took place with one of my clients and a close personal friend of his. With their permission, I have documented their conversation. Their names are fictional.

My client (Ed) suggested that his friend (Tom) consider working with a personal Coach. Tom asked my client (Ed) the following questions:

Tom: *In what ways has your Coach assisted you?*

Ed: My Coach has given me an opportunity to think out loud about my business without fear of repercussions, and I found many times just by talking through issues that are concerning me the answers became evident. I also found that my Coach, because of her lack of familiarity with the subject matter, would ask me often the simplest questions that would give me different insight into the situation.

Tom: *What has been most important to you in working with your Coach?*

Ed: The additional personal insight I have gained as a result of our in-depth discussions.

Tom: *For example?*

Ed: I was considering an individual for an appointment to a key position, which would allow our company to expand more in the international marketplace. Since the individual had been with me for some time, my Coach asked why I had not already placed this person in the new position. I replied I was not confident that I could give this person 100% of my trust. She then asked me, what had changed? Then it became clear that nothing had changed. I simply was selling myself that this person was right for the position, and I realized what I was doing. As Jack Welch would say, I wasn't facing reality.

Tom: *What have you learned from your Coach that you could not have learned from your friends and associates?*

Ed: First, I am much more comfortable in talking with a person outside of my business and circle of friends. I feel I can be much more candid and will get unbiased feedback. I have many friends and business associates that I can and do seek guidance and counsel from, however, I cannot be totally open and share personal and confidential information.

Tom: *How did you find a good Coach?*

Ed: First, it is not easy because the use of personal Coaches is not widely practiced amongst CEOs and other top-level executives. I personally found my Coach through the recommendation of another Coach.

Tom: *How did you determine your Coach was right for you?*

Ed: In our initial interview I developed very specific questions that would give me insight into this person's attitude, character and interest. For example, I think that one factor that is especially important is that your Coach must be totally candid with you and not tell you what he or she thinks you want to hear. For example, one of the questions I asked the Coach was, "How do you determine if a prospective Client is someone you truly can help?" This enabled me to find out if the Coach had selection criteria or was accepting anyone that would pay the fee. If your perspective Coach does not have selection criteria, then you can assume they are only interested in the fee.

Tom: *What experience and background should a Coach have?*

Ed: The Coach certainly needs to have experience in the business world, including exposure to top-level executives. The more personal experience a Coach has with interaction of top-level executives, the more insightful that person is. An example might be Peggy

Noonan, who is a journalist and former speechwriter of President Ronald Reagan. She has a depth and wealth of experience and knowledge that she brings to any discussion. Therefore that top-level experience is vital, in my opinion. I am not saying that every personal Coach should be like Peggy Noonan, but she is an example of some one who is current, informed and open to new learning. Naturally, you want a Coach who has boundaries, integrity and a genuine interest to serve.

Tom: *What monetary value would you place on what you have received from your Coach?*

Ed: I am not sure there is any monetary value that I would place on the benefits that I received from my personal Coach. I know that the ROI on my investment of time with my Coach is many times whatever fee I pay. I just wish I'd have the same rate of the ROI on my other investments…

Even though this conversation could be considered open and direct, Ed did not disclose personal details of his coaching experience, specific issues relating to two of his Board members and a very difficult family situation. These subject matters are too private for him to reveal to even one of his closest friends.

In my experience of coaching CEOs, I learned to appreciate the value of having a clinical and psychological background. Not only does this help the Coach to recognize more quickly any pathology such as depression or any other mental disorder, it also provides for the additional use of a range of therapeutic skills deriving from a counseling history such as 'deep' listening. Deep listening refers to the ability to 'hear' and sense the client's feelings and not just pay attention to the actual content of the communication. This intuitive ability allows the Coach to connect with the client on a Soul level, where the issues of spiritually-based leadership can be addressed.

A Coach who is grounded and solid in his or her own spirituality will be comfortable in dealing with powerful individuals and not be intimidated by them. This Coach will have the strength and confidence to ask the tough pertinent questions without faltering.

A non-judgmental, non-preconditioned position of a Coach brings a freshness to the creative coaching process that is, as Ed mentioned in his conversation with Tom, of great value.

Traits that all CEOs appreciate in a personal Coach are fast thinking, a good sense of humor and wit. I recall some of the most impactful meetings included fun and some good belly laughs. Last but not least, a CEO wants to know that his or her Coach is winning in life and lives by his or her own principles. That's what really gives respect and credibility to a Coach in their eyes. Given the complex and unique personality profile of a CEO and the important role they play not only in their organization both nationally and internationally. It is an awesome job. Therefore, a CEO Coach offers a most important service that in fact touches many people's lives by assisting leaders on their spiritual journey.

Key Points

- **Personal coaching is skyrocketing in popularity and acceptance, even among CEOs and other top-level executives.**

- **Coaching is a cost-effective and valuable catalyst for both personal and business transformation.**

- **Working with a Coach is intimate, personal and totally confidential.**

- **In selecting a Coach the most important steps are to review his or her credentials, life and work experience and skills.**

- **A decision to work with a Coach is highly personal and based upon the integrity of both people involved.**

- **A CEO Coach must have exposure to top-level executives.**

- **A Coach who is grounded and solid in his or her own spirituality has the strength and confidence to ask tough pertinent questions without faltering.**

- **A CEO Coach offers a most important service that touches many people's lives by assisting leaders on their spiritual journey.**

PART II
OUR MULTIDIMENSIONAL SELF

Chapter 1
Our Source

A man who writes of himself without speaking of God is like one who identifies himself without giving his address.

Ben Hecht

We are multidimensional beings, Soul/Spirit entities. Pure Spirit is non-material and a part of God, our Creator; it is consciousness, love and bliss, as told to me by Spirit Guide Theobald. This is something we cannot fully comprehend. As human beings, we enjoy a multiplicity of emotion and body, feelings, intellect, thinking and Soul and Spirit. As some New Age gurus preach, however, we are NOT God. True spirituality is not commercialism and superficial spirit-entertainment. Since the beginning of time, charlatans, merchants and entertainers, sometimes in the disguise of prophets, ministers, Mediums and spiritual leaders, have sold *"God"* with great success.

Theobald adds that *Multidimensional living means living your life as a human fully and without restrictions. Don't try to be superhuman and deprive yourself of all experiences that are normal and healthy. This includes all feelings and physical experiences such as pain and pleasure. Being multidimensional also means to be accepting of others and their different life styles. In addition, it means to gain increasingly more knowledge and understanding of spiritual laws and to live accordingly. It includes foremost the ability to be present in the moment, which means to have faith in the good and God's divine, right plan, without worrying about tomorrow.*

Some have turned true spirituality, our very core, into a ridiculous, dangerous shallowness. Contrary to what might be preached in books, magazines, radio and television, true spirituality is not even primarily about ourselves. It is equally about focusing on and helping others.

When we choose to follow a spiritual journey that will truly lead us back to God, we always have two areas of focus: the inner quest and service to others. This journey is hard and may take a long time. It may involve questioning and struggle, loneliness and uncertainty. We may be forced to evaluate our religious or non-religious upbringing, to wrestle with the problem of evil, to look at our own failings and fears, our mortality, our relationships. This, however, does not mean that spirituality is a dark and grim process. True spirituality can be joyful, fascinating and even fun.

The journey ultimately leads to love, something for which everyone is so hungry. It is not easy to accept delayed gratification, to work hard and deny ourselves quick pleasures. Nor is it easy to deny instant fixes, distractions or "more important" priorities, which serve to feed our egos and desires for material goods and fame.

Originally, we were pure Spirits. Now we are trapped in this dense costume of sorts, our physical body. A friend of mine witnessed the birth of her newborn grandchild. When he finally entered the world, this child had "an expression on his face from another World that moved me to tears," she said. "I knew he was not quite here yet, on this planet. And then, within a few minutes, he began to cry." At this moment she became acutely aware that we all are from someplace else, and as such, have a divine connection to the Universe.

What is our Soul? There are many answers, and yet we still don't know exactly what it is. We can, however, make a connection with our Soul through our intuition or gut feeling. Gary Zukav, author of *Seat of the Soul,* talks about the multidimensional personality. He believes that we actually have one additional sense beyond the traditional five, a sense that he likens to an intuitive kind of knowledge. He claims we are born with this sense.

I spent many years asking myself the question: "Why are we having a human experience? Why are we here?" According to Theobald, *we are here to learn and to school our Souls because we have moved astray from God. We have given in to greed, selfishness, envy and the misuse of material goods and power.* Theobald tells us that when we first arrived on this planet, we actually had two more senses that have since disappeared over hundreds of thousands of years because of negativity and self-absorption. Not very flattering to our narcissistic spiritual super egos! One of these lost two senses is the kind of intuition that animals still have, the ability to sense things that are going to happen (for example, an earthquake) or the ability to discern whether someone is a positive or negative person. Most of us have lost that sense.

Additionally, we have lost the sense of telepathy, which now only more intelligent beings on other planets have. Yet it can be argued that some of us do have this telepathic ability with special people in our life. At a recent Tabula Spiritualis Meeting in Victoria, BC, over 90 percent of the attendees reported telepathic experiences.

Make no mistake, to be fully human is very difficult and represents an ongoing challenge. We live with adversity, polarities and paradoxes daily. Many of us are searching to find and connect with our source. Despair, loneliness and alienation are common today as we build our spiritual foundation. The Spirituality industry is booming. Elizabeth Lesser, in the publication SCIENCE of MIND, March 2001, identified warning signs for today's spiritual seekers. She warns about the danger of *Spiritual Narcissism* as a fine line to "following your bliss." Practices of superficiality and sentimental shallowness tempt you to surround yourself with trivial phrases, such as hollow affirmations or ritual objects, which can range from the outright silly and ridiculous to the serious.

Spirituality becomes another escape. "Without some degree of sacrifice for the greater good, self-discovery eventually leads to plain old self-indulgence," Lesser says. Sometimes people will simply take another seminar or read another book just to avoid dealing with the difficult choices and actions everyone has to make. New research confirms we are attracted to "magic" more than ever. We are also likely to romanticize spirituality rituals from other cultures.

One of the most attractive aspects of the currently popular spirituality craze is shameless grandiosity. Healers, preachers and channellers are emerging everywhere. Many become messianic little Popes, humorless saints or just unbearably profound individuals, grander or better than other people. It appears that most of us remain like sheep, not leaders, and blindly follow these ever changing and newfound charlatans (gurus, preachers, therapists and yes, coaches) more for self-serving egotistical needs and vanity than for learning about life's deeper purpose.

When Theobald was asked about the value of life as a hermit, he replied *while this was certainly not a harmful thing to do, it would not advance us much spiritually, either. Actively doing something, like building a hospital for sick children, for example, would help our spiritual development much more.*

Interest in spirits, angels and other forms of intelligent life is rising dramatically. According to a recent pole in *USA Today,* 81 percent of the people in the U.S. believe in heaven as a place where they will live with God after they die. Ninety-one percent believe in angels; 88 percent believe they will meet family members and friends again; 63 percent believe in Hell, and about 30 percent believe in some sort of purgatory. The evidence for Spirit existence has been present from antiquity to modern times.

Confucius and other philosophers, thinkers, classic writers and researchers, including Plato, Aristotle,

Cicero, Plutarch and Maximus of Tyre frequently spoke and wrote about Spirit existence as an established fact. Even Shakespeare, Milton, Tennison, Longfellow, Blake, Goethe, Thomas Mann and many others wrote with clear authority about the continuing life of man. At the First Multidimensional Congress-Th. in Victoria, BC, Canada, Co-Chair Roy Chitwood reminded the audience of Rudyard Kipling's famous poem "The Sack of Gods":

...They will come back – come back again,
As long as the red earth rolls.
He never wasted a leaf or a tree.
Do you think He would squander souls?"

The Old and New Testament, together with every other major religious scripture, are filled with references to Spirit communication, both verbal and visible. The Rev. Dr. George Searle, Rector of the Catholic Church of St. Paul in New York City, said, "In our times no one denies the existence of spiritualistic facts, except a few with their feet firmly on Earth and their brains in the moon... Anyone who considers the manifestation of them as mere humbug, trickery or delusion is simply not up to date."

Even the Bible provides numerous references to Spirit existence, for instance 1. Cor. 15, 44, 46. The evils of possessing Spirits are referred to again and again in the Old and New Testament. (See 1 Samuel 16:23; Matthew 10:1; Mark 1: 39; Luke 8:27, 16:18, 29:36; Acts 19:12; Mark 9:17, 9:21, 9:25, 9:27.) Even the well-known physicists, Kip Thorne and Stephen Hawking, are even wondering why we have not yet met people from our own future.

There are unimaginable possibilities of God's creations, of which we are an important part. There is a massive amount of literature about aliens, UFOs and alien abduction. Much is speculation, fiction or a combination of both. To give an example of the vastness and mostly incomprehensible phenomena, here are some facts:

- The overall statistics of documented UFO sightings are currently over 111,500 worldwide.
- Generally speaking, scientists distinguish between two main categories of aliens: Class A and B. Two-thirds belong to Class B, mostly round forms of light sightings without permanent structure that appear suddenly, disappear and appear again. They can divide themselves in half and then melt together again. The more interesting UFOs are considered those of Class A. They consist of a variety of unknown artificial flight objects (or ships) with metallic-like structure. While those flight objects of Class B could, in fact, be explained as fine-material or "natural" phenomena, the UFOs of Class A represent real flight vehicles, which can and, as we know now, do carry passengers.

The issues relating to UFOs are just one of numerous aspects of the complexity and variety of many mysteries in our life. As Dr. Michael Hammer writes in *THE AGENDA,* "An insistence on certainty and clarity is the absolute killer of progress." Many of today's leaders are aware of these unexplained phenomena and are humbled by the recognition of the inaccessible comprehension of such creations. It becomes clear to them that life in the Universe is not by chance but by design. Based on the knowledge that there is a 'Designer,' a Spiritual Source, a Creator, they can support, encourage and foster the further advancement of our human abilities and research, while ensuring responsible and ethical conduct.

KEY POINTS

- **We are multidimensional, spiritual beings.**
- **When we choose to follow a spiritual journey that will truly lead us back to God, we always have two areas of focus: the inner quest and service to others.**
- **True spirituality can be joyful, fascinating and even fun.**
- **It is not easy to accept delayed gratification, to work hard and deny ourselves quick pleasures, instant fixes, distractions or "more important" priorities, which serve to feed our egos and desires for material goods and fame.**
- **As human we have lost two senses, which we had over hundreds of thousands of years ago: an instinctual sense of intuition and telepathy.**
- **There are unimaginable possibilities of God's**

creations, such as UFOs and extraterrestrial intelligent life, of which we are an important part.

- Leaders who have recognized the connection to our true source can support, encourage and further advancement of our human abilities and our spiritually-based ethical conduct.

PART II
OUR MULTIDIMENSIONAL SELF

Chapter 2
The Challenge of Our Soul/Spirit/Body Connection

A human being is a part of a whole, called by us, the Universe, a part limited in time and space. He experiences himself, his thoughts and feelings, as something separated from the rest — a kind of optical delusion of his consciousness. This delusion is a kind of prison for us, restricting us to our personal desires and to affection for a few persons nearest to us. Our task must be to free ourselves from this prison by widening our circles of compassion to embrace all living creatures and the whole of nature in its beauty.

Albert Einstein

Your Soul allows for the connection to your *source* made through intuition, or what we call "gut feeling." Soul and body are the gradual materialization of your pure Spirit-self.

"The mysterious presence we call God endlessly renews the revelation of itself through nature, history and the human soul," says Rocco A. Errico, Th.D., Ph.D., author and founder/president of the Santa Fe, New Mexico-based Noohra Foundation. It is ignorance, lack of education, arrogance and/or just stupidity to say that there is no God or divine order. Evidence of His creation of the Universe or other life forms, e.g. Spirits or other extraterrestrial intelligent life forms in the Universe, is everywhere.

The ultimate challenge is to integrate, take care of, protect and honor our Soul, Body and Spirit. Our awareness of our multidimensional existence, our Spirit and Soul entity, our unique vibrations and biochemical and physical energy fields, our memories and changes all make up our total Self. We are increasingly rediscovering our once lost spiritual abilities. We need to relearn old skills and acquire new ones so we can be more fully who we are meant to be. Most of these skills are down-to-earth, practical and include:

- The hygiene of our physical, ethereal body and mind
- Recognition and management of positive and negative forces
- Accurate identification of cues from our intuition
- Working with "White Light"
- Proper use of mental activity
- Opening and closing of our Chakras
- Affirming positive thoughts and statements daily
- Calling our Spirit Guide and other spiritual helpers for guidance and protection
- Clearing our homes, cars and offices of negative energy or Spirits
- "Dialoging" regularly with God, our Spirit Guide or Guardian Angels
- "Drowning" fear and worry into the bottom of the ocean

- Mentally removing ourselves from the activities of the world in order to become still and centered
- Continually seeking knowledge (such as The Konzern, see Glossary)
- Respect and management of more subtle boundaries (such as avoiding reckless interference by disrespectful and ego-driven Mediums)
- Recognizing death as a transition to a continuum of life
- Allowing the dead to be dead and helping them through their transition (without clinging to them through our pain of loss)
- Support and value the work in hospices.

Dr. Elisabeth Kübler-Ross, noted expert on death and dying says, "There is a right time to die. Listen to the dying person! Let them die where they want to die. Doctors have been trained to feel like failures when a patient dies." She teaches the importance of helping the dying to leave this earthly plane with dignity and compassion.

Corpses, advises Theobald, *should not be cremated for at least three days after clinical death, as burning destroys most learning and consciousness. When that happens, our consciousness that is materialized can be destroyed, and spiritual lessons have to be learned again in a new reincarnation.*

Recognize that in life there is divine providence and free will. At the same time, there are unpredictable events, such as "accidents" or plane crashes. When a body is destroyed through sudden injury due to fire or explosion, a Soul is often in confusion and remains earthbound, not knowing where to go or where it belongs. The Soul tries to find another body through which it can express itself. You don't have to be an "Exorcist" to help those lost ones to move on. Talk to them. Tell them they are dead, and that everything is all right. Encourage them kindly, yet firmly, "to go to the Light."

This kind of spiritual activity, which could be declared as non-logical and therefore easily be dismissed by an only rational thinking individual, could be more understood in the context of the discovery of different types of intelligence. At the beginning of the twentieth century, as psychologists discovered ways and means to measure intelligence, Aristotle's definition of man as "a rational animal" developed into an obsession with the IQ (Intelligence Quotient). In the mid-1990s, author Daniel Goleman popularized research into the Emotional Intelligence Quotient (EQ), pointing out that EQ is a basic requirement for the appropriate use of IQ. According to Oxford-based authors, Dahan Zohar and Dr. Ian Marshall *(The Quantum Self, The Quantum Society, Who's Afraid of Schrodinger's Cat?* and *Rewiring the Corporate Brain),* there is collective evidence from psychology, neurology, anthropology and cognitive science that there is a third "Intelligence," which is "SQ" or the Spiritual Intelligence Quotient.

Unlike IQ, which computers have and EQ, which exists even in higher mammals, SQ is uniquely human and, according to Zohar and Marshall, the most fundamental of the three kinds of identified intelligence. It is linked to humanity's need for meaning. SQ is what we use to develop our longing and capacity for **meaning,**

vision and **value.** It allows us to dream and to strive. It underlies the things we believe in and the role our beliefs and values play in the actions we take. It includes the shape we give to our lives. The indications of a highly developed SQ include:

- The capacity to be flexible (actively and spontaneously adaptive)
- A high degree of self-awareness
- A capacity to face and deal with suffering
- A capacity to face and transcend pain
- The quality of being inspired by vision and values
- A reluctance to cause unnecessary harm
- A tendency to see the connections between diverse things (being "holistic")
- A marked tendency to ask "Why?" or "What if?" questions and to seek "fundamental" answers
- Possessing a facility for working against convention
- Being what psychologists call "field-independent."

A person with a high SQ is also likely to be a servant leader — someone who is responsible for bringing higher vision and value to others and has the ability to show them how to use it. In other words, this is a person who inspires others. We live in a spiritually-dumb culture characterized by materialism, expediency, narrow self-centeredness, lack of meaning and a dearth of personal SQ. We can raise our SQ by asking "Why?" questions and by looking for the connections between things. It's important to become aware of the assumptions we have been making about the meaning behind and within things.

Daily practices, such as meditation, simply being still or reading a poem or a couple of pages from a book, will improve communication with one's self. Reflecting on "why" questions, going for a walk, taking one's mind off busy goal-oriented activity with some kind of "time out" allows us space in which to think. We may want to listen to a piece of music or keenly notice some scene or event from the day, and go over it later in our minds. We may look for the more subtle nuances and associations in the world or keep a diary in which we recall not only the events of the day, but also our dreams and how to responded to them and why.

At the end of each day, we may contemplate. What were the activities and experiences that struck or affected us the most? What did we enjoy about the day? What do we regret? How could the day have been different? How could we have felt or behaved differently, and what effect would that have had? These are activities that will help raise our SQ.

Our spiritually-dumb culture seldom forces us to face our personal edge but cocoons us with ready distractions and easy options. A very central part of self-awareness involves recognizing the boundaries of your comfort zone. This is another way of asking, where is your edge? What is that place on the edge of your personal or work relationships or activities where you have to stretch yourself? Where you are challenged? Your edge is your growing point, the place from which you can transform yourself.

In Nietzsche's book *Thus Spoke Zarathustra,* he announced the death of the old order. He wrote, "One must have chaos in one to give birth to a dancing star. I tell you, you do have chaos in you." What Nietzsche meant by "chaos" was the ability to self-organize, to re-invent, to go beyond the traditional categories of good and evil that have been imposed by top-down religions.

The heart of the spiritually intelligent Self is, according to Zohar and Marshall, ultimately a quantum vacuum, the ground of being itself. It is a still and changing ground, and the heart that knows it is both. SQ is a deep form of spontaneity; a response to the deepest core of the Self and to the core of being in which that deep Self is grounded.

SQ appears paradoxical and is therefore difficult to understand. Yet when deeply spontaneous, we are naturally in connection with our own inner Self and with all others who are a part of that Self. We are connected with all of nature and its processes and with the whole of universal reality that is a part of that Self. Then we know that we are the World and thus are accountable for it. We take responsibility for others because we respond to others, as they are a part of us.

Key Points

- **Soul and body are the gradual materialization of our pure Spirit-self.**

- **The ultimate challenge is to integrate, take care of, protect and honor your Soul, Body and Spirit.**

- **Help the dead in their transition.**
- **Be more fully who you are, relearn old skills and acquire new ones.**
- **Develop your third "Intelligence," "SQ," or Spiritual Intelligence Quotient.**
- **Stretch yourself to your edge, the place from which you can transform yourself.**
- **Know that you *are* the World, and take responsibility for it.**

PART III
THE SEVEN SECRETS

Chapter 1 — The Seven Secrets

SECRET 1: Being "Fully" Human

"To be fully human means having faith and doubts, living and loving fully and having freedom."

"Theobald" Spirit Guide

What do we need to do to be "fully human," not only to accept, but also to embrace **all** of our human experiences? That includes sexuality, family, community, play, work, consciousness, awareness and knowledge. It means learning to manage life's polarities, adversities and paradoxes as well as embracing all our roles of mother/father, friend, lover, judge, listener and decision-maker. This is what leads us to becoming spiritually enlightened and fully human.

Unlike animals, we have the ability to experience "courage." Courage comes from the heart. The heart is in the center of our human body and directly connected to the Soul. Courage can be conscious and unconscious. It can have its roots in our multidimensional origin, our inherited part of our Soul, but it can also be learned. Behavior-oriented psychology validates that courage can be learned on a conscious level with the help of one's children, parents, friends, therapists, coaches, spouse and mentors.

Knowing that we are a lot more than what we see and that everything is based on vibration, we already know a number of effective ways to look after ourselves. To keep our energy field "clean" and within a high level of vibration, we know how to use a number of previously mentioned proven practices. This includes recognizing the body as a precious gift to be cared for with responsibility.

According to psychologist, philosopher, lecturer and author, Nathaniel Branden, Ph.D., only by taking responsibility for ourselves can we have any *real* power over our lives. He stresses the critical roles of self-responsibility, self-reliance and personal autonomy in the development of healthy selves. Today's world, according to Branden, needs men and women who are willing to think, to be self-directing and self-managing, to respond to problems proactively rather than passively waiting for someone else to "do something," to be initiators and innovators. In *Taking Responsibility* (Simon & Schuster), Branden delineates four goals that relate to choice:

- To illuminate the meaning and implications of self-responsibility as a way of living and of being in the world;
- To show that this practice is not an enormous burden but a source of joy and personal power;
- To establish that we create ourselves — shape our identity — through what we are willing to take responsibility for; and

- To demonstrate that self-responsibility, self-reliance and individualism are essential to the well-being of our society.

It is appalling that the vast majority of the New Age teachers attempt to convince people that all they have to do is sit quietly in a corner and visualize success. Absolutely not! When we have a vision held with passion, it is a physical experience. It's an emotionally felt drive, which compels us to be active and to create. It is about making a plan and taking appropriate action step-by-step. That's when we feel energized and fully alive! That is what brings success.

It's not just sitting and visualizing, and perhaps silently holding resentment that "everybody else is successful and I am not." Nor is it a "moan-and-complain" session that is sometimes disguised as a 'spiritual meeting' or 'group therapy session,' fostering, for example, hatred toward people with money. *"Money is not intrinsically dirty. It is energy, God's energy. But we have to use it wisely and with responsibility.* According to Theobald, *God does not want us to live in poverty; God wants us to experience abundance. He wants us to do well and to enjoy luxuries. We are meant to enjoy material things and to enjoy human activities and interaction, to have the human experience with everything, fully and in freedom.*

Theobald cautions, however, that *we have to work for it.* This is not an easy planet on which to live. *It is considered by the Spirit World to be the lowest in the Universe.* This planet is full of adversity, craziness, struggle, confusion and uncertainty. To some, this world appears to have nothing but limits and frustration. Is it any surprise that people are often defensive, self-protecting and fearful? Most people live their lives fearing loss or an inability to get what they want.

Sadly, this fear is the very thing that stops people from experiencing true happiness, joy or serenity. Almost everyone experiences anxiety, angst or fear at some time. It is a common human experience. Can you learn to stop being afraid? If yes, how? First, recognize the fear. Fear can be such a habit that it is often kept hidden from one's self. Hidden, it is often disguised as a lack of courage, problem with authority, jealousy and envy, rigidity, the inability to speak up, stinginess, lack of assertiveness or the inability to achieve success in a chosen career. Fear is all about limiting one's self by not understanding that love is something that flows beyond limits.

It might be argued that choice comes before courage. Although courage, to some degree, can be learned through example and reinforcement, this is a kind of courage that is non-learned. It is a kind of primal drive that we bring with us as Souls from other lives and from previously acquired learning. This courage is not necessarily conscious, but it relates to inner wisdom. In children, this wisdom is sometimes very present, even startling.

By way of illustration, consider the following study on human behavior conducted at the University of Minneapolis in the mid 1980s. It involved male twins in their early 40s. One of the twins was a very well-adjusted family man and businessman, a communicative person who enjoyed a good marriage and children. The other had been in and out of jail at least 10 to 15 times. This twin drank heavily and refused to take responsibility for his actions.

By testing each of the twins independently, the goal was to learn what traits they shared and what traits they did not have in common in order to understand what contributed to the vastly different outcome of their lives. At first, nothing of consequence surfaced. Then, they were each asked to explain what they believed contributed to the type of person they turned out to be. Both gave the same answer, "Because my father was an alcoholic."

Here the issue of choice is so obvious. One chose to use his father's horrible life to get his act together, to live well and to do the right thing, whatever that meant to him. The other used that same reason as an excuse for victimization. He just "reacted" by sabotaging his life.

We also bring with us a certain predisposition as a Spirit-Soul entity. Depending on the state of our Soul in our previous incarnations, we bring this additional asset with us. While these men had very similar physical bodies, their Souls were very different.

There are numerous people who are deeply depressed or unhappy who cannot find a connection to any early childhood or current life situation to warrant their ongoing, unhappy feelings. Their distress happens on another level. For example, I recently met a woman who complained of constant depression, yet even by her own admission, could find no reason for it. She enjoyed good parenting as a child, and as an adult, a good life with not only loving relationships and physical health, but also financial stability. There was nothing relating to any sexual problem.

She herself had never dealt with any poverty, major illness or loss, yet she was miserable and tended to cling to her possessions. She was very stingy and paranoid and was obsessed with cleaning everything around her excessively. She was unable to be alone and needed to keep busy at all times. She hoarded material things and renovated her house again and again. When she ran out of things to do, she traveled. I realized she was a very disturbed Soul, one that held hatred, disbelief and negativity. I knew that unless she addressed her relationship with herself on a very different level, a spiritual level, she would not improve.

Today she has made some progress. She made the choice to look inward, to review her spiritual position and to practice faith. She has become much more quiet and calm. She still has work to do, but at least her fears have decreased. She has become a little more generous with family members and has become more comfortable being alone.

Often, with an understanding therapist, healer, good friend or mentor, people can become aware and make a conscious decision to change. Being a "victim" or "martyr" does have payoffs in the form of short-term satisfaction or gratification. They get to "be right," and the world feels sorry for them. This, after all, is not such a bad thing since it offers some kind of short-term validation. People typically change only when the payoff ceases to be enough. Until that happens, people rarely say, "Okay, I'm ready to learn. I'm ready to *really* take on life." If it weren't such a major attraction to be a victim, we certainly would have far less of them, and our society wouldn't support them.

Victims are usually "angry" people with their anger rooted in fear. They tend to alienate themselves from others, thinking that no one in the world cares. It is self-fulfilling because anger alienates people so that, yes, no one is there to love them. When a person is finally willing to break through the anger, the grief, sadness, loneliness and fear, the experience can be overwhelming. In many cases, the fear of death is at the core of loneliness and anxiety. In other situations, fear is about life itself, who you are, why you are here, your Soul/Spirit/God connection and the painful, lack of self-acceptance and self-love.

Learning to love is about boundaries, good manners, self-discipline, commitment, responsibility and respect. You need to learn to esteem your Self. How? In my experience, there are two main building blocks for acquiring self-esteem: keeping your word and giving to others. When you say, "I will meet you at 5:00 P.M.," and you don't, you break your word primarily to yourself and secondarily to the person you are meeting.

Self-esteem is typically underestimated, misunderstood and approached too superficially. When you build a history of keeping your word and doing good for others or helping someone else or a group of people, you build confidence in yourself. The self-lesson is that you are reliable and therefore trustworthy, which produces value. You have reason to respect yourself and hold yourself in high regard.

Being "fully" human means having self-respect and

self-esteem, and that comes from your commitment to achieve maturity. This requires positive action. Living the sheltered life of a nun or priest or being a 'spiritual' recluse does certainly not hurting anyone. On the other hand, this choice may not provide the tools that enable us to really advance as humans in a more powerful way.

In reality, those hermits who are considered enlightened may not necessarily be any more enlightened than a common individual. For example, consider the life of a simple shoemaker who brings up five children, works hard to provide for them, cares for his ill wife and does so diligently despite his sore back. He may be more spiritually enlightened than the professional "Light-seeker" even though he is not well educated. As Theobald says, *Enlightenment is invisible to humans.* We tend to confuse spiritual enlightenment with what we call character, status or talent and judge it by external, measurable accomplishments. In the extreme, avoiding our immediate responsibilities by hiding out where we are protected and safe might even be considered self-indulgent and, to some degree, self-centered.

Rather than by climbing to the top of the mountain, enlightenment can be found in one's own backyard. Putting energy into developing an ethical corporate environment, for example, or simply being kind and considerate to those around us and helping wherever we can, enhances the Soul's development. Enlightenment **is action.**

KEY POINTS

- **Accept *all* of your human experience.**
- **Keep your energy field "clean."**
- **Be self-directing and self-managing; respond to problems proactively.**
- **Hidden fear is often disguised as a lack of courage, problems with authority, jealousy and envy, rigidity, the inability to speak up, stinginess, lack of assertiveness or the inability to achieve success in a chosen career.**
- **Fear is about limiting one's Self by not understanding that love is something that flows beyond limits.**
- **Learn to esteem your Self by keeping your word and giving to others.**
- **True enlightenment is action.**

SECRET 2: Boundaries

"The one who sets boundaries can also cross them occasionally without falling back. The one setting these boundaries does not need to be afraid to cross them once in a while, since he knows what they are. The one who does not set boundaries is simply like a savage in the jungle, crossing them all the time without limits, even if it brings him to his ruin."

"Theobald" Spirit Guide

Boundaries. You do **not** have to spend three days with your Mother if she's not good for you. You **can** limit the length of your visit. There are ways to manage your life so that you're not affected by negative aspects, even those aspects that cannot change, such as the personality of someone who is toxic to you. Martyrs are demanding, needy and narcissistic people without a sense of boundary. They are draining. Boundaries are vital to keeping us healthy. They are a way to recognize and pay attention to one's own needs. When someone enters a room and makes you feel a little funny, don't just dismiss it. Pay attention. Recognize, of course, that it could be you who hasn't had a good night's sleep. Perhaps you are the one being cranky and grumpy or having negative, miserable thoughts. But just maybe, you are picking up on something that you would otherwise dismiss. Pay attention, be aware, and move around it.

People can be just like leeches or vampires, often disguised in very nice packages. They may appear as helpless individuals to whom your heart goes out. You want to wrap them up in a silk blanket and comfort them. They can evoke a sense of nurturing inside of you, which will only deplete you. Also, they can show up as competent, cultured executives with an apparent understanding of mankind and its challenges, who in reality, are only all too eager to rip your company's morals apart with their shark-like teeth. Defining your boundaries is a crucial aspect to achieving personal and professional well-being and happiness.

Happiness **is** a **choice.** Sometimes this choice needs to be made again and again. Whenever you find yourself on a dead-end street in your life, in a toxic relationship or if you have just lost track of where you're going, pause and reevaluate your situation. What do you do? Re-commit to your choice for happiness. Once your decision is made again, mountains suddenly become smaller.

Some people struggle with this concept their entire life. Maria, a young mother who experienced sexual, emotional and other physical abuse, comes to mind. Growing up in South Africa, she lived through war, poverty and violence. Now thirty-five years old, her marriage is falling apart, and she has four children to raise. Her own mother, a highly regarded woman in the community, was the main abuser, even though she was admired by everyone for adopting sixteen children.

What was Maria's first step? She realized she had a choice. Her goal was to heal her many emotional wounds and grow more confident. She knew she needed much courage, and she decided to HAVE it. Courage sometimes comes only after a goal is clear — the kind of profound courage that directly relates to faith, knowing deep in your heart that you are divinely guided and protected.

How do you connect to your faith in your desire to HAVE courage? Through silence. Simply be still, so you can think clearly and turn inward into your core, your heart. Mentally, you can always call on your invisible Spirit helpers and ask them for guidance and protection. They are there instantly.

Setting boundaries from a spiritual, not only worldly perspective gives an added element of strength and empowers anyone in leadership. Leaders, who operate with this additional awareness and make positive use of this knowledge will be more in tune with their intuition, are more centered and most likely more creative in making their decisions.

Key Points

- **Practice spiritual and emotional hygiene by setting and recognizing the importance of boundaries.**

- **Happiness and courage are choices.**

- **Be still, so you can think clearly and turn inward into your core, your heart.**

- **Leaders who make positive use of their knowledge of spiritual dimensions of boundaries are more effective.**

SECRET 3: Authenticity and Character

Authenticity: *... being entitled to acceptance or belief as being reliable, genuine, real, principled, having authority*
Character: *... sum of mental and moral qualities, being distinctive*

The Oxford Dictionary of English Etymology

Authenticity has its roots in the Soul; however, as humans we still must make an effort to connect with this part of ourselves with sincerity and commitment. Authenticity is about being clear on what is most important to you **and** living it. This involves having courage and character, our innate ability to make decisions and a willingness to stand alone and separate, if necessary.

In Atlanta, early November 2001, US President Bush called in his Presidential Address upon the citizens of the World to build character and decency by building communities of service. In our current state of global threats and terrorist activities, ancient virtues suddenly have come again to the forefront of our consciousness and human responsibility.

In conversations with unhappy individuals, I've often heard them say, "I feel so far removed from God." The truth is God hasn't moved, so who has? In his book, *The Ethics of Excellence,* Dr. Price Pritchett addresses the concept of personal responsibility. Consider this (edited) passage:

Where the Buck Stops

Notice that "I" is at the center of the word "ethical." There is no "they." Achieving the ethics of excellence is our individual assignment.

We've got to get past the idea that somebody else is supposed to fix things — like "top management," the politicians, our justice system, the schools, or even our religious institutions. These faceless groups don't exist except through the lives, the day-to-day behavior, of common people like you and me.

Who is this vague *"they"* we blame for so many of our problems? "They" is the obscure party we use as our whipping boy to camouflage the fact that we — you and I — and other specific human beings, just like us have to start doing things differently. "They" can't fix anything. We can.

But when we get enough people who don't care, and who don't accept personal responsibility for high ethical standards, our organization gets the "M" disease: *Mediocrity*. Anybody can be a carrier.

By the same token, every individual can carry the cure.

Much has been written about discovering who we are. While not discounting the information that's already available, the reality is that we can never fully comprehend who we are. This is because of our multi-dimensionality and our many histories. While we typically don't have direct access to information regarding past lives, a quality Medium can help to identify a few experiences from the past that will enable people occasionally to move forward.

Knowledge about previous lives will be a fragment, a fraction of information about our whole existence. What is happening post-natally is clearly of most importance for the evolution of one's Spiritual self in this lifetime and throughout eternity. Therefore, the commonly used phrase, "I need to find myself" is a waste of time. While this perspective sounds spiritually noble and perhaps even admirable, in reality it is simply a convenient and often used excuse to not move ahead and to avoid some important decisions that need to be made. It's a trap into which many people fall. What is most important is to **think,** to be clear on what is most important **and** doing something about it.

At one point in my life, I realized I was stalling in making some important, painful decisions. I believed I just had to "take another seminar for self-improvement," instead of facing up to my fears and discomfort. Similarly, a man I know left his wife and two children and went to Nepal for two years because he wanted to "find himself." Two years later, he came back, and the only thing he found was that he lost his family.

New Age Psychology has a very elaborate, eloquent

and convincingly seductive vocabulary. But when we look closely at its followers' lives, their relationship patterns and their willingness to confront their personal issues with courage and honesty, we find that it is for the most part, a scam.

Our job is not to "find ourselves," but to identify our core values. If you don't know what they are, here is a simple remedy. Think about what is most important to you, and write down your values. Now apply them, and move forward as though they are the "right" ones. Then pause periodically to evaluate, think, learn, adjust and move ahead again. This is a start. Life, after all, is a journey of trial, error and discovery. Even with the best clinical assessment, psychological aptitude tests, business plans or proven strategies, we need to be flexible and open, constantly adjusting, re-evaluating and re-directing ourselves. Things will happen that for which we haven't planned, and as such, will present new insights and learning we haven't thought of previously.

Key Points

- **Authenticity is about being clear on what is most important to you and living it.**
- **Virtues like courage, character, decency and commitment are again in the forefront of our consciousness.**

- **Face your fears and discomfort.**

- **Be alert to and not be seduced by New Age Gurus who attempt to convince you to avoid confronting your responsibilities by spending time "to find" yourself.**

- **Identify your core values.**

- **Accept that life is a journey of trial, error and discovery, learning — and effort.**

SECRET 4: Mental Power

Success is hastened or delayed by one's habits. It is not your passing inspirations or brilliant ideas so much as your everyday mental habits that control your life. Habits of thought are mental magnets that draw to you certain things, people and conditions. Good habits of thought enable you to attract benefits and opportunities. Bad habits of thought attract you to materially-minded persons and to unfavorable environments.

Paramahansa Yogananda

"Positive thoughts produce positive results, and negative thoughts produce negative results," says Dr. Norman Vincent Peale. It is obvious that proper thinking most likely leads to proper behaviors, and improper thinking to improper ones. More advanced spiritual teachers from the East, for example, have been known for their mental powers for a long time. Unfortunately, the ability to manifest through thought is still highly unrecognized today.

Thoughts appear to precede feelings. For example, you cannot easily *feel* unhappy unless you have just had a negative or unhappy thought prior to that feeling. The timing involves fractions of seconds. And since we are more than the operation of our brain, we have the ability to learn to direct and manage its activity — our mental power. We know that thought is energy. If we have many of the same thoughts repeatedly in alignment, they form a density of vibration, which will dramatically accelerate its materialization and bring positive or negative results. Need convincing? Just think about the many recent findings pointing to the effectiveness of prayer. When using passion and visualization, enriched by all of the five senses, it is especially potent.

Professors Peg Thoms and Dawn Blasko of Penn State Erie University, Pennsylvania created a very exciting tool called the "Visioning Ability Scale." It develops and measures a leader's ability for positive imaging. They use exercises and coach executives to strengthen their power to create a strong vision for the organization.

"Since the function of leadership is to produce change," writes Harvard Business School professor John Kotter in his classic article, "What Leaders Really Do" *(Harvard Business Review,* May-June 1990), "setting the direction of that change is fundamental to leadership." "Setting the direction," he continues, "is not the same thing as long-term planning. It is more inductive. A leader crafts a vision that describes what a business should become over the long-term and lays out a feasible way of achieving this goal."

The constructive, positive use of mental power can be learned. It can be learned by anyone. The problem, however, is that people want to have it easily, without expending any effort. This just doesn't work. In my experience, it requires a strong commitment and tremendous self-discipline to develop that mental power of focus and clarity.

Everyone, including children, needs heroes who radiate strong positive thought. We are inspired by them and depend on these individuals to lift our spirits and to ignite a life vision for which we deeply long. We need them because heroes, just by being, communicate the ideal, yet realistic picture that we can turn our lives into something great. The key, of course, is to have the right heroes, to be lifted by greatness and not just by glamour, to be lit by the desire to do good as opposed to the desire to do well.

Key Points

- **Proper thinking leads to proper behaviors and improper thinking to improper ones.**
- **Thoughts appear to precede feelings.**
- **Everyone, including children, needs the heroes who radiate strong, positive thought.**
- **The constructive, positive use of mental power can be learned by anyone.**
- **A strong commitment and high self-discipline are required to develop the mental power of focus and clarity.**

SECRET 5: Beauty and Play

Beauty is but the sensible image of the Infinite. Like truth and justice it lives within us; like virtue and the moral law it is a companion of the soul.

George Bancroft

As a student attending the University of Cologne in Germany, I spent an entire term collecting scientific data on the role that esthetics play in emotional well-being. Again and again, we proved there were positive emotional and physiological changes in people who surrounded themselves with selected types of music, art and poetry or simply spent time in nature. These people knew how to look for and recognize beauty.

Connecting consciously with beauty aligns our energy fields and contributes dramatically to our well-being and healing. Ideally, every facet of life should contain an element of beauty, clarity and pleasure. To bring esthetics into our world can be as simple as lighting a candle during dinner, pruning a tree or cleaning one's desk. Even Tom Peters, one of the most popular business gurus today, who is not only known for his intellectual brilliance, but also for his somewhat provocative, arrogant style, stresses the importance of the presence of beauty in every project in his book *The Brand You 50.* World-class fashion designer Christian Dior says, "zest is the secret of all beauty and that there is no beauty that is attractive without zest." Beauty is not static. In its presence, we feel alive.

Play, like beauty, is about free flow and movement. Beauty and play are closely connected. Like beauty, play is active and moving. In play there is an alignment, an order of sorts, though not necessarily in a linear sense. Creativity, freedom, spontaneity and laughter are manifestations of play. It is a mental attitude and a way of being that does not always require planning or a special time set aside for that purpose.

Often, as adults we don't play, or we may have forgotten what play is. We have many activities, hobbies, recreations and interests, but we don't play. Even when we run, we don't run as children do. We "work" at running, or we "work" at recreation and therefore are not *re-created.*

The essence of play is also the real essence of intimacy — something we don't know much about anymore. True intimacy is not about doing. It's a way of being. We continue, however, to go from activity to activity in search of play, just as we tend to go from person to person in our quest for intimacy.

The experience of joy, however, can only occur when we are relaxed and not stressed or on overload. While sitting quietly in a busy airport, for example, we can suddenly have a profound recognition of gratitude or sense of joy that rushes through our body. This can happen quite spontaneously. It is a sense of indescribable delight. Physically, it is a sort of tingling. According to Tom Robbins, Cosmic/Comic and American author, "Joy itself is a form of wisdom. If people are nimble enough to move freely between different perceptions of reality and if they maintain a relaxed, playful attitude well-seasoned with laughter, then they would live in harmony with the Universe; they would connect with all matter, organic and inorganic, at its purest, most basic level."

Theobald tells us there is a lot of joy, play and beauty in the Spirit World, however, mostly with those Spirits close or on their way to God. He points out that their joy and delight are beyond our comprehension. Happiness on the highest spiritual level, he says, is so intense that it is unimaginable for us. It would make us wonder if we had gone "crazy." He also reminds us that while everything striking and beautiful does *not* always equal "good," good is always beautiful.

Beauty and play are vital ingredients of successful living and successful enterprises. In my experience, I have seen that truly successful people live this truth.

Key Points

- **Look for and learn to recognize beauty.**
- **Beauty and play are closely connected.**
- **Play, like beauty, is about free flow and movement.**
- **The essence of play is also the real essence of intimacy.**
- **Beauty and play are vital ingredients of successful living and successful enterprises.**

THE SEVEN SECRETS

SECRET 6: Openness

"Questions are Knowledge, and Knowledge is Power."
"Theobald" Spirit Guide

My most profound personal experience, thus far, has been my contact with my Spirit friend, Theobald. The information I have received has been extraordinary, but I had to be open to receiving this information for it to have been of such value in my life. What I mean by being open is more than pursuing ongoing education and training, which are without question a continual task for any leader. Being open also requires more than "out-of-the-box" thinking. Being open means being receptive to the unthinkable, unimaginable and improbable.

It is also understanding and accepting the fact that we know very little. Even though one's SQ or Spiritual Intelligence Quotient is currently considered the "ultimate" intelligence, we may yet discover another, and yet another, even greater type of intelligence in the very near future.

Since my first contact with Theobald in 1995, I have formulated and asked several thousand questions of all types and documented his answers. I have spent several sleepless nights during the past six years attempting to digest the information I received while, at the same time, developing more questions. At times, I was frustrated and painfully aware of how little I was able to comprehend with my brain. Theobald's reminders that many truths and concepts are not comprehensible with our limited human brains were no consolation for me.

Despite the many concepts I may never fully understand while I am in this body, I do know that since meeting Theobald, my learning curve has multiplied many times. As strange as it may sound, Theobald had become my primary mentor and coach. Today I know that the information he provides will be published in the near future and will have a major impact on those who are open to it.

Openness is also more than the ability to communicate, even more than really *hearing* the other person. In his book, *Getting The Love You Want,* Dr. Hendrix offers a valuable communication model, called "Conflict Dissolving" as opposed to "Conflict Resolving," a popular technique in the past. Conflict resolution involves primarily a left-brain approach to identifying the pros and cons of a problem and finding a mutual, sensible and logical resolution.

Conflict dissolving is the creative outcome of a communication process that allows the parties to really "hear" each other, their intent, their feelings and their position, without analyzing the objectives from a predominately logical perspective. This process helps to defuse the emotional charge that often makes communication difficult, painful and ineffective. It helps the parties to stay focused on the overall good will and tends to "dissolve" emotional roadblocks that are in the way of getting to a positive resolve.

Used with good intent, this along with many other techniques, can be powerful and transforming. Like many recognized therapeutic skills, educational or coaching models, however, their usefulness is limited.

Nevertheless, if applied with the awareness that there is much more to man and his whole make-up than can ever be fully addressed, we can place them into a useful perspective. Perhaps just knowing that would help any professional to be a better and more humble therapist, physician, teacher, coach or business leader.

Being open and modest regarding our awareness, *not* knowing all the answers, gives us, in a paradoxical sense, the "competitive advantage" over those who know it all. By realizing our limitations, we actually make room for new possibilities.

Key Points

- **Be open and receptive to the unthinkable, the unimaginable and the improbable.**
- **Understand the wisdom of knowing that we know very little.**
- **Many truths and concepts are not comprehensible with our limited human brain.**
- **Openness is more than the ability to communicate, even more than really *hearing* the other person.**
- **Realize your limitations and therefore new possibilities.**

SECRET 7: Unshakable Faith

To one who has faith, no explanation is necessary. To one without faith, no explanation is possible.

Saint Thomas Aquinas

There has always been an abundance of hope in the World. Especially after the terrorists' events of September 11th, most everyone is hoping for World peace. The poor hope to get rich; the sick hope to get well; the sad hope to gain happiness, and the troubled hope to find inner peace. Everybody is hoping for something, but few have the faith necessary to manifest that "something." What we need is more faith.

We hope that our prayers will be answered, but sometimes we can be so absorbed that we fail to notice the answer. To have hope is like looking at the door, but never opening it. To live in hope is like dreaming the great dream, but never moving forward. Hope remains stationary.

The concept of faith, which is vastly different than hope, is difficult to grasp and to define. Yet it plays such a dominant part in our life. Faith is an inner knowing that there is meaning to life. It is a conviction that there is a continuum of life after our physical death and that everything is already all right. Unlike hope, it is active.

Two years ago one of my clients was experiencing total chaos in his personal and professional life: bankruptcy, divorce, major litigation, alienation from two of his key business associates, the death of his mother and his son's car accident. In the midst of his turmoil, he amazed me with his statement: *"...but I know, Anneli, everything will work out. God is looking after me."* And so it was.

Today my client has had more than one miraculous turn for the better. Shifts and solutions appeared that no one could have anticipated or thought of at the time. The intelligence and creativity of Divine Guidance are beyond our imagination. The faith of this individual, his deep "knowing" of his "Divine Guidance," cannot be communicated fully through reason and logic alone. Therefore, there is no conventional "proof" of this truth to a limited, solely intellectual mind. It appears that the intellectual form of truth generally has little power; it is the inner spirit of truth that gives life, freedom and enlightenment.

Most everyone I have met has experienced pain, confusion, grief, doubt or even despair at least once in life. It is during these times that our faith is challenged the most. As difficult as it may be to comprehend, these times can bring us closest to God. As we go through life's darkest moments, when we feel lost and question our deepest beliefs, we can connect with and feel God's love and compassion. How can this be? It is possible because we are Spirits, and if we open ourselves up to God, He will respond. We know that even in moments of greatest despair, we are never alone.

In our spiritual lives, our awareness of suffering, injustice and crime increases over the years. We become more sensitive and fine-tuned to the sorrows of the World. How else can we appreciate the sweetness of joy if we do not know the bitter taste of sorrow?

For most of my adult life I have passionately argued in private circles and in public situations that Evil does not exist. I was convinced that Evil is ignorance and that it came from simply not understanding who we really are as humans and denying our source. I thought this ignorance was, at least in part, a lack of intelligence. When I debated this subject with Theobald, he responded that certainly intelligence, as humans understand it, is not equated to goodness. In fact, he said intelligence and goodness are not necessarily even connected. He asked me to look around with open eyes, so that I could see plenty of evidence that Evil forces were at work. As US President Bush stated, the results of the September 11th terrorists' attacks were a result of evil forces. Theobald reminded me that it is often the uneducated, simple man *"whose hands show cuts from working in the field,"* who is *"the most humble and spiritually advanced Soul."*

For us as humans, it remains a challenge to recognize the truth while facing adversity, poverty, unattractiveness or paradox. We like God to look good. To this point, Reverend Sage Bennet, Ph.D., who is co-dean of the Los Angeles-based Homes Institute and has worked with the poor for many years, said in an article in *Science of Mind* in March 2000, "It is certainly easier to see God in the guise of beautiful parks and lakes than it is in the grimy face of a homeless man who wants to wash our car windows for spare change."

According to a 1999 article in the *New York Times Magazine,* 96 percent of Americans do believe in God. The words "In God We Trust" are printed on US dollar bills. Many of the founding fathers of the world's nations acknowledged God as the Creator and the source of universal love and goodness. Yet when we study the Universe, our minds are overwhelmed by its vastness. If we attempt to encompass and comprehend God only on a mental or conceptual level, we produce the same mind-boggling experience as when we attempt to mentally encompass our immense Universe.

Our interpretations of God *must* then fall short of what God is, because we can only describe this invisible Spiritual essence and presence in terms of what is known. Trying to explain God only through His creations known to us would be like trying to explain the existence of the sun through one of its rays. "God" is indescribable in physical terms or ideas; because God is more than *any* of the concepts we can hold and will always remain a mystery to the rational thinking mind.

Today, there is an increasing need to address our relationship with God and life itself in order to experience true happiness. When we ignore the issues of our Soul and our relationship with God, our inner happiness will remain elusive. We need to commit to self-discovery and connect with the depth of our Spiritual truth in order to touch and experience the essence of the "good." Only then will we know what we as humans have in common, our real roots and recognize that arguing about "why my God is better than your God" has no place.

There is an order in the Universe much bigger than what we can ever imagine. It gives us direction. When we truly know that we are living in eternity **right now** and have purpose because we **know** of our true source, life becomes easier and more like a playground filled with wonder and excitement.

Learning the right balance of allowing flow and exercising right action is the ultimate mastery of everyday living. This is something I personally want to learn and accomplish in this life, and yet it is something I still struggle with more often than I would like to admit. For me, self-patience is difficult.

God is filled with love, and God gives us free choice. If we abandon God, however, over and over and over, eventually there will be a place of no return. How else could we explain the essence of the law of cause and effect, as well as the essence of real justice?

Total recognition of one's Self as a multidimensional, spiritual being with utmost Divine purpose and responsibility, given life by one single Creator, God, is what will give us ever-increasing true confidence, genuine joy, love and happiness. Rooted in our solid, unshakable inner knowing, our faith in the "good," we can achieve Ultimate Success, which will in turn, positively influence all aspects of human life.

Key Points

- **While there is an abundance of hope in the World, what we need is more faith.**

- **Hope is stationary, and faith is active.**

- **Faith is an inner knowing that there is meaning to life.**

- **The faith of "knowing" of "Divine Guidance" cannot be fully communicated with reason and logic alone.**

- **The inner spirit of truth will give us life, freedom and enlightenment.**

- **The most challenging times can bring us closest to God.**

- **Learning the right balance of allowing flow and exercising right action are the ultimate mastery of leadership a well as of everyday living.**

- **The recognition of one's Self as a spiritual, multidimensional being, created by one God and the faith in the overall good will give us ever-increasing confidence, genuine joy, love and happiness.**

PART III
THE SEVEN SECRETS

Chapter 2 — Conclusion
TRUTHS I LEARNED AS A THERAPIST AND COACH

He is the wisest who seeks God.
He is the most successful who has found God.

Paramahansa Yogananda

While sitting in a dentist's chair a couple of years ago, I decided to focus my thinking on something other than the pain, the sound of the drill, the smell and the various activities surrounding my mouth. I chose self-reflection and asked myself what life's most important lessons had been. The thoughts that came to me were so clear. As soon as my procedure was over, I quickly returned to the waiting room and jotted down my answers on a nearby napkin.

Later, when I shared these life's Truths with my dear friend, Liz, she urged me to develop my thoughts and write a book. While I never saw myself as a gifted writer, I decided to follow her suggestion and wrote this book. Here are the notes I wrote on the napkin that day in the dentist's office. They represent the original seeds of my work as well as its completion.

- All distress, pain and/or illness are governed by the Law of Cause and Effect.
- The value of analysis and the search for 'WHY?' are often overrated. It is better to identify what is most important and to establish and follow a plan of action.
- We need to control our minds (intellect) and not allow our minds to control us.
- We are more than our intellect. Our intellect is a great student but makes a poor master.
- The key and starting point to resolving any relationship issue is to communicate with and strengthen one's relationship with ONESELF.
- It is more important to be kind than to be 'right.'
- The issue of fear or terror cannot be resolved without addressing our relationship with God.
- Acceptance is more important than understanding.
- The individual's process of spiritual development and maturity has two focuses, the inner journey and serving others.
- Self-confidence is the ongoing process of knowing you can *and* will keep your agreements, the experience of true courage, however invisible it may be to others and making a contribution.
- Commitment, respect, love and humility are the most empowering of all virtues.
- The purpose of life is learning.
- We all need to learn the same lessons; however, their sequence and the individual's journey are uniquely different.
- Faith is more important than reason.
- We have freedom of choice and action — always.

As a therapist and Coach, I have come to understand these basic Truths about real fulfillment, inner peace, beauty, abundant joy, faith and ultimate success. I also know there will be more understanding and new insights as I continue to live on this planet, and I will continue to share my knowledge with others as long as I live. *"ULTIMATE SUCCESS – 7 Secrets to Spiritually-based Leadership* will forever change your thinking about leadership and your important role you play in many people's lives. From the depth of my heart, my wish for you is that you achieve the ultimate success, both personally and professionally, and the happiness you are longing for in this lifetime.

Suggested Reading

Nathaniel Branden Ph.D. *Taking Responsibility: Self-Reliance And The Accountable Life* (Simon & Schuster, 1997) **Written for people who are willing to think, be self-directing and self-managing.**

David D. Burns MD. *Feeling Good: The New Mood Therapy, Vol.1* (Morrow William & Co., 1999) **How to unlearn negative and ineffective thinking patterns and get rid of depression, procrastination, self-criticism and many other self-depleting, yet cherished, bad habits.**

Roy E. Chitwood CSP, CSE *World Class Selling: The Science of Selling – The Complete Selling Process* (Best Sellers Publishing, Minneapolis, 1999) **Comprehensive book on the process of selling based on integrity and state of-the-art strategies; includes taking the mystery and fear out of selling.** *www.maxsacks.com*

Daniel Goleman *Emotional Intelligence* (Bantam Books, Inc., 1997) **Introducing a vital trait of effective leadership with applications.**

Steven M. Greer MD. *Extraterrestrial Contact: The Evidence and Implications* (Crossing Point Inc. Publications, 1999) **Regarded as one of the World's foremost authorities on the subject of extraterrestrial intelligence (ETI), Greer gives an inside view of briefings with the U.S. President, key members of Congress, the UN leadership and Pentagon officials at the highest military level.** *www.cseti.com*

Stanislav Grof *Psychology of the Future – Lessons from Modern Consciousness Research* (State University of New York Press, 2000) **Offers direct experiential and empirical evidence that spirituality is a critical and legitimate attribute of the psyche, which is not in conflict with science.**

Michael Hammer Ph.D. *THE AGENDA – What Every Business Must Do to Dominate the Decade* (Crown Press New York, 2001) **A current. practical, no-nonsense guide to business success in the 21st century.**

Harville Hendrix Ph.D. *Getting the Love You Want: A Guide for Couples* (Harper Trade, 1989) **Brilliant discovery of the relationship connection, which allows for hands-on strategies to build happy and fulfilling relationships.**

Patrick Lencioni *The Five Temptations of a CEO – A Leadership Fable* (Jossey-Bass Inc., 1998) **Leadership-traps are well presented.**

John E. Mack MD. *Passport to the Cosmos – Human Transformation and Alien Encounters* (Crown Publishing Group, 2000) **As esteemed professor of psychiatry at Harvard Medical School, Mack presents a controversial study about alien abductions and other cosmic mysteries.**

Wolfgang Matthias *My Wife – The Un-Known Medium* (Soon to be published in German) **Introduction to a new Worldwide Spiritual Consciousness: The Konzern – In Accordance with God and the Spiritual World.**

M. Scott Peck MD. *The People of the Lie – The Hope for Healing Human Evil* (Simon & Schuster, 1997) **Very controversial, Peck courageously addresses the issue of Evil, which many of our popular New Age Gurus consider only as a fiction of our imagination.**

Tom Peters *The Brand You 50: Fifty Ways to Transform Yourself from an 'Employee' into a Brand that Shouts Distinction, Commitment, and Passion!* (Alfred Knopf, 1999) **Short, pointed, compelling; how to be a leader in your own industry.** *www.tompeters.com*

Price Pritchett Ph.D. *The Ethics of Excellence* (Pritchett and Associates, 1998) **Carving out an organization's character through daily choices and shaping its conscience as though it's one's own; practical, simple, straightforward advice.**

Lee Pulos Ph.D. and Gary Richman *Miracles & Other Realities* (Omega Press, 1990) **Fascinating account and documentation of so-called "paranormal" phenomena, which will be recognized by the informed reader as natural energy-based occurrences.**

Ulrich Friedrich Radtke, Manuela Matthias, Ruth Mohacsi *Between Heaven and Earth – A Dialogue with The Incomprehensible* (Soon to be published in German) **A revolutionary and stimulating documentation of new knowledge about the phenomena of cosmic events, the history of Earth and mankind, physics, mathematics and the science of natural healing.**

Ralph Waldo Trine *In Tune With The Infinite* (Woolnough Bookbinding Ltd. Northampton, UK, 1995) **First published in 1899, this book is a classic on spiritual knowledge and wisdom.**

Bennet Wong MD. and Jock McKeen MD. *A Manual for Life* (PD Publishing, 1992) **Most comprehensive and practical guide for self-mastery and self-reflection.**

Nancilee Wydra *Feng Shui – the Book of Cures: 150 Easy Solutions for Health and Happiness in Your Home or Office* (NTC Publishing Group, 1996) **Clear, concise guide to a complex and complicated topic.**

Danah Zohar and Ian Marshall Ph.D. *SQ – Spiritual Intelligence: The Ultimate Intelligence* (Bloomsbury Publishing, 2000) **Introduced after IQ and Goleman's EQ, SQ is a new, third type of intelligence that is uniquely human and linked to meaning, values, vision and more.**

Gary Zukav *The Seat of The Soul* (Simon and Schuster Trade, 1989). **Renowned physicist recognizes that authentic power does not come from the intellect but from the "Heart," a multidimensional aspect of the "Self."**

BIBLIOGRAPHIES AND OTHER RESOURCES

Sage Eileen Bennet "Living Wisely: 10 Points That Link," *Science of Mind,* March 2000

Jim Braham "The Spiritual Side: CEOs SPEAK UP about how spirituality helps their companies, employees, customers – and themselves." Executive Life, *INDUSTRY WEEK,* February 1, 1999

Rocco Errico Th.D., Ph.D. "The Divine Name," *Science of Mind,* February 2000 & "God's Name" December, 1999

Matthew Fox "Religion 2000! An Interview with Matthew Fox," by Roger Juline, *Science of Mind,* August 2000

Steven M. Greer MD. *Extraterrestrial Contact: The Evidence and Implications* (Crossing Point Inc. Publications, 1999)

Stanislav Grof *Psychology of The Future. Lessons From Modern Consciousness Research* (State University of New York Press, 2000)

John Kotter "What Leaders Really Do," *Harvard Business Review,* May-June 1990

Patrick Lencioni *The Five Temptations of a CEO: A Leadership Fable* (Jossey-Bass Inc., 1998)

Elizabeth Lesser "Warning Signs for Spiritual Seekers," *Science of Mind,* March 2001

Michael Maccoby "NARCISSISTIC LEADERS: The Incredible Pros, the Inevitable Cons," *Harvard Business Review,* January-February, 2000

John E. Mack MD. *ABDUCTION: Human Encounters with Aliens* (Macmillan Publishing Company, New York 1994)

Peggy Noonan "Three Presidents. One Lesson." *Wall Street Journal,* Feb. 9, 2001

Norman Vincent Peale *The Power of Positive Thinking* Simon & Schuster, 1987

Carol S. Pearson *The Edge Book of Practices: Things YOU Can Do to BRING SPIRIT TO WORK,* Innovision Communications, Aliso Viejo, CA, 1999

Marcia Penkins-Reed "Committing," *Science of Mind,* September 1994

Price Pritchett Ph.D. *The Ethics of Excellence,* Pritchett & Associates, Inc., Dallas, Texas

Jennifer Wohl "The Heart of Faith: Common Threads of Spiritual Traditions," *Shared Vision Magazine,* December 1999

Paramahansa Yogananda *THE LAW OF SUCCESS: Using the Power of Spirit to Create Health, Prosperity, and Happiness, Self-Realization Fellowship,* Los Angeles, CA, 1980

Danah Zohar and Ian Marshall Ph.D. *SQ – Spiritual Intelligence: The Ultimate Intelligence* (Bloomsbury Publishing, 2000)

Gary Zukav "The Journey Toward Authentic Power," by Walt Murray, *Science of Mind,* February 1990

www.theobaldkonzern.com

www.manuela-das-medium.de

ORDER FORM

ULTIMATE SUCCESS

7 Secrets to Spiritually-Based Leadership

By

Anneli Driessen Ph.D, CMS, MCC

CEO Coach

Name ______________________________

Organization ______________________________

Address ______________________________

City, State ________________ Zip Code ____________

Country ____________ E-mail ________________

Phone ________________ Fax ________________

Please send me _____ copies.

Price: $28.95 CDN or $19.95 US

Add $9.55 CDN or $7.55 US (Tax and Shipping & Handling).

Add $3.00 per book for multiple orders.

I am enclosing $ ______ for the total purchase price.

Please send check or money order — no cash or c.o.d.'s — to:

Anneli Driessen
1516 Louise Place
Victoria, BC, Canada V8P 2T9
Tel. 250-472-0909
Fax 250-721-4296
anneli@annelicoach.com
http://www.annelicoach.com

Phone and email orders can be charged by Visa.

TRUTHS ***I have learned as a Therapist and Coach:***

- All distress, pain and/or illness are governed by the Law of Cause and Effect.
- The value of analysis and the search for 'WHYs?' are often overrated. It is better to identify what is most important and to establish and follow a plan of action.
- We need to control our minds (intellect) and not allow our minds to control us.
- We are more than our intellect. Our intellect is a great student but makes a poor master.
- The key and starting point to resolving any relationship issue is to communicate with and strengthen one's relationship with ONESELF.
- It is more important to be kind than to be 'right.'
- The issue of fear or terror cannot be resolved without addressing our relationship with God.
- Acceptance is more important than understanding.
- The individual's process of spiritual development and maturity has two focuses, the inner journey and serving others.
- Self-confidence is the ongoing process of knowing you can *and* will keep your agreements, the experience of true courage, however invisible it may be to others and making a contribution.
- Commitment, respect, love and humility are the most empowering of all virtues.
- The purpose of life is learning.
- We all need to learn the same lessons; however, their sequence and the individual's journey are uniquely different.
- Faith is more important than reason.
- We have freedom of choice and action — always.

Anneli Driessen Ph.D., CMS, MCC
CEO Coach